# PARIS

## THE STORY OF A GREAT CITY

# DANIELLE CHADYCH & DOMINIQUE LEBORGNE

ANDRE
DEUTSCH

**PREVIOUS PAGE** A souvenir medal commemorating reaching the top of the Eiffel Tower in 1889 by the engraver Charles Trotin.

**RIGHT** A drawing by Marie-Pierre Monnier of the Café des Deux Magots and the Church of Saint-Germain-des-Prés (6th arrondissement).

# Author's Acknowledgements

The authors would like to thank the following people for their help with this book:
Olivier Accarie-Pierson, Benjamin Arranger, Alain Aymard, Yvan Bourhis, Lionel Britten, Jean-Marie Bruson, Marie-José Dassas, Nathalie Dassas, Maryse Goldemberg, Roselyne Hurel, Charlotte Lacour-Veyranne, Odile Le Fur, Gaëlle Lemaire, Jean-Marc Léri, Geneviève Madore, Florian Meunier, Geneviève Morlet, Jeanne Ozbolt, Mélanie Petetin, Dominique Revellino, Sylvie Robin, Myriam Siméon, Philippe Sorel, Dominique Titeux, Jocelyne Van Deputte, Sylvie Vermeulen, Chantal Viellart, Véronique Voignier, Jean-Baptiste Woloch.

This is an Andre Deutsch book

Text © Danielle Chadych & Dominique Leborgne, 2010, 2014
Design © Carlton Books Limited 2010, 2014

This edition published in 2014 by Andre Deutsch
A division of the Carlton Publishing Group
20 Mortimer Street
London
W1T 3JW

First published in 2010

Printed in China

A CIP catalogue for this book is available from the British Library

ISBN: 978 0 233 00438 9

# CONTENTS

RIGHT A poster by Jules Chéret (1836–1932) for the Palais de Glace in the Champs-Élysées, 1894. This skating rink was situated at the corner of the Avenue des Champs-Élysées and the Avenue Franklin-Roosevelt in the 8th arrondissement and was open from 1892 to 1980.

# INTRODUCTION

With 27 million French and foreign tourists each year, Paris attracts more visitors than any other city in the world. From its modest origins as the provincial town of Lutetia it has blossomed into a capital city with international appeal, thanks to its architecture, museums, gardens, cafés and bustling vitality.

Paris is relatively compact compared with other capitals, as its 2,201,578 inhabitants live in an area of 66 square miles. Situated on the River Seine, it enjoys a favourable position on a very busy north–south communications route. The pace and nature of its development depended on a series of defensive walls, which were built between classical times and 1920, apart from a hundred-year period or so between 1670 and 1785.

Paris is the product of centuries of history and bears the imprint of each successive epoch. From the Middle Ages to the nineteenth century, kings, queens and emperors built defensive walls, palaces, bridges and fountains; they founded churches and the university; they encouraged the creation of plots of building land and they opened hospitals, markets and schools. François I, Henri IV, Louis XIV, Napoléon Bonaparte and Napoléon III all took a particularly keen interest in making the capital look more attractive. However, the "Princes of the Blood" (legitimate male descendants of royal dynasties), members of the Court, high ranking members of the clergy and army officers – all of whom lived close to the sovereigns – created a boom in residential building. Provosts, prominent citizens, the middle classes and ordinary private individuals helped by architects, craftsmen and engineers all played their part in giving Paris its multifaceted appearance. The monumental works of Napoléon III transformed the city, enriching it with numerous edifices. Since the end of the nineteenth century, the presidents of the Republic have made efforts to enhance the prestige of the capital.

Victor Hugo was captivated by the city, dedicating a chapter to it entitled "A Bird's Eye View of Paris" in his novel, *The Hunchback of Notre Dame*: "Linked by a similarity in taste, style and bearing to each of these characteristic monuments are a certain number of houses scattered around various quarters that can be spotted and easily dated by an expert eye. When one knows how to look, the spirit of a century and the features of a king can be found, even in a door knocker."

*Paris: The Story of a Great City* takes the reader on a voyage of discovery of the city's past, providing a chronological account of how the events that unfolded in the capital intersected with the wider history of France. The presentation of the City of Light's key monuments, as well as the inclusion of some twenty facsimile documents, enhances the tale of this great capital city.

**LEFT** A panoramic view of Paris from the top of Nôtre-Dame Cathedral.

# The Origins of Paris

Lying at an average altitude of 26 m (85 ft) above sea level, Paris is surrounded by hills such as Montmartre and Belleville, both of which rise to about 128 m (420 ft). The course of the city's river, the Seine, has changed with the passing centuries. In the prehistoric period around 10,000 bc, the Seine was disproportionately powerful in relation to its actual flow. It more or less followed the route of the Grands Boulevards, hugging the hills of Belleville, Ménilmontant and Montmartre as far as Pont de l'Alma. During exceptionally high water at one point, the Seine abandoned its meandering curves to follow the straight line that it still takes today. When Paris experiences terrible flooding, approximately once every hundred years, the Seine tends to revert to its old course. This is what happened during the Great Flood of 1910, when Gare de Lyon and Gare Saint-Lazare were under water, although they lie far away from the river. Nowadays, in spite of various protective measures along the Seine (locks, reservoirs and raised embankments), the city still dreads being flooded.

**ABOVE AND TOP RIGHT** Images from a booklet of photographs published to commemorate the Great 100-Year Flood in Paris between 28 January and 15 March 1910.

**OPPOSITE** This watercolour of the rue Maître-Albert in the 5th arrondissement by Louis Perin (1871–?) shows the floods of Paris in 1910. They began on 21 January, reached their apogee on 28 January and ended on 15 March. Parisians were forced to use boats and canoes as their means of transport.

Between 9,000 bc and 500 bc, people gradually began to settle in Paris. Nomads established a temporary encampment on the banks of the Seine during the Mesolithic Period (9,000 bc). As hunter-gatherers, they pursued game such as boars, stags and roe deer. Evidence of this can be seen in the remnants of hearths and arrowheads found at 62 rue Henry Farman in the 15th arrondissement. The weapons that these hunters preferred to use were bows and arrows, but the heads made of flint, a durable material, are the only parts that have survived.

The site of Paris was occupied on a permanent basis from the Neolithic Period, which began in 4,500 bc, until the dawn of the Iron Age in 500 bc. For 4,000 years, people lived in riverside pile dwellings at Bercy (now Quai de Bercy in the 12th arrondissement), navigating the river in dug-out canoes. They were farmers who raised livestock, but continued to hunt, gather wild berries and fish for carp and pike. They carved and polished bone and flint, and made pottery containers. In about 4,000 bc, people settled on the site of what is now the Louvre, where traces of farming and funeral rites have been discovered.

**ABOVE** Bifaces such as this were used as tools for a number of tasks: they could cut wood and also be used as a weapon against animals or enemies.

**RIGHT** A model of Paris and the surrounding area during prehistoric times made by Laurent Renou. During the prehistoric period, the course of the Seine River curved more and deployed more to the north than it does nowadays.

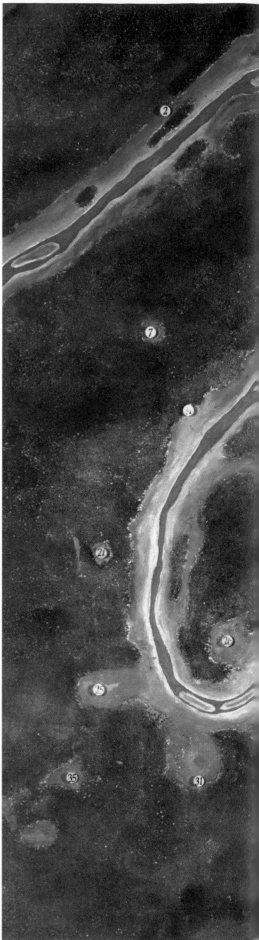

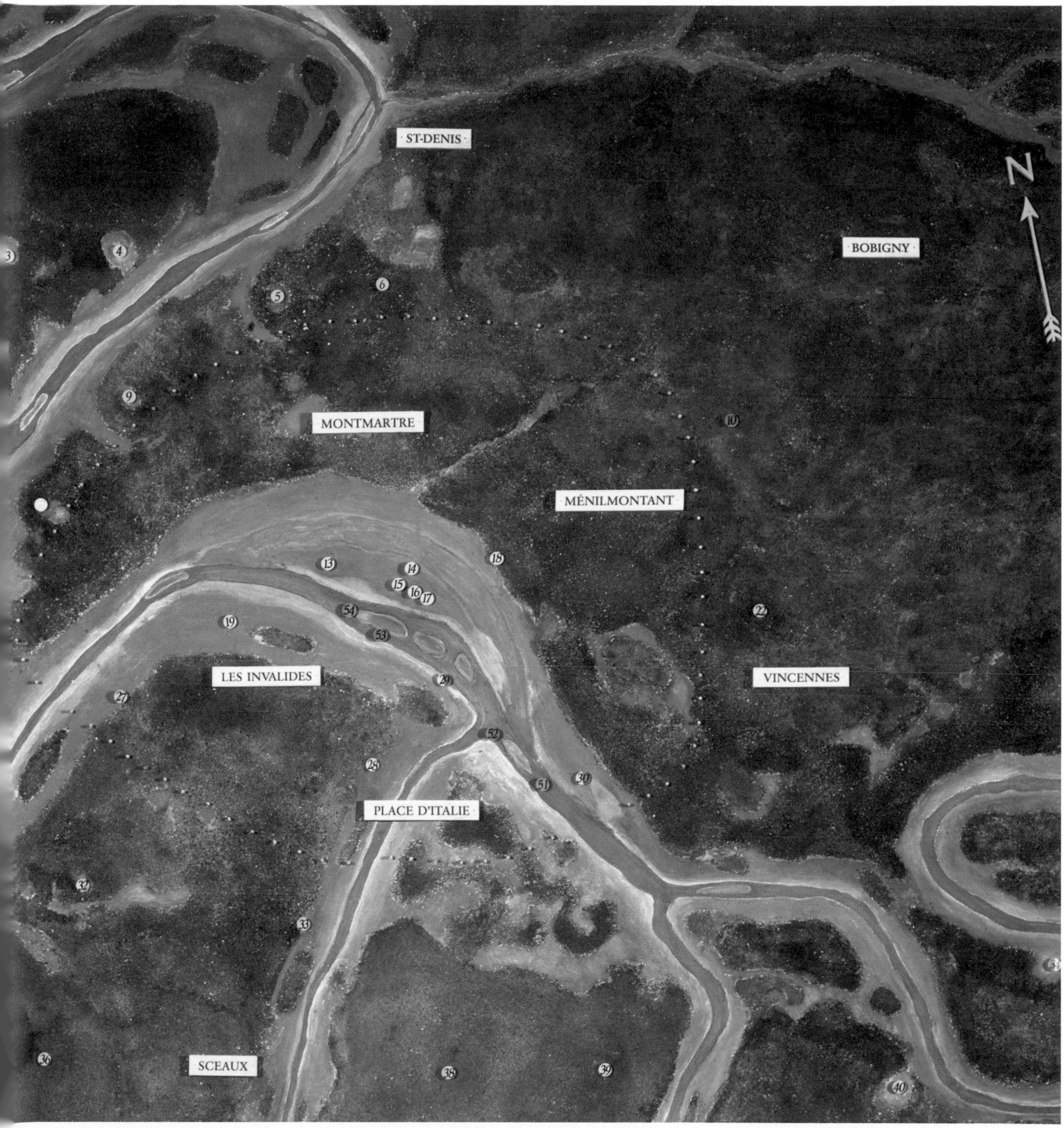
ST-DENIS
BOBIGNY
N
MONTMARTRE
MÉNILMONTANT
LES INVALIDES
VINCENNES
PLACE D'ITALIE
SCEAUX
3
4
5
6
9
10
13
14
15
16
17
18
19
22
27
28
29
30
32
33
36
38
39
40
(51)
(52)
(53)
(54)

We do not know the exact location of the main settlement (*oppidum*) of Lutetia, the forerunner of Paris. For a long time historians believed that it was located on the Île de la Cité, but no Gallic remains have ever been discovered there. Although foundations of huts have been uncovered, suggesting the presence of a temporary structure on the site, they do not offer proof of permanent urban development. The only evidence we have to locate Lutetia in Gaul lies in Julius Caesar's account of the Roman conquest of Gaul (now France) in *Commentarii de Bello Gallico* (*Commentaries on the Gallic War*).

In 52 BC, the Parisii, a small tribe that settled around Lutetia, joined Vercingetorix, who united the various Gauls fighting against the Roman invader. To suppress the Parisii's revolt, Julius Caesar sent his lieutenant, Labienus, to Lutetia, which he described as "an *oppidum* of the Parisii situated on an island in the Seine". Lutetia was defended by Camulogène, the Gallic chief who practised a scorched earth policy, setting the city on fire and destroying the wooden bridges. Labienus succeeded in tricking the Gauls' defenders and engaged them in the Battle of Lutetia, which ended in the death of Camulogène and the defeat of his army. Vercingetorix, beaten in Alesia in 52 BC, surrendered to the Romans.

Pinpointing the location of Lutetia on the Île de la Cité is a matter of controversy, especially since Caesar was not there in person and did not give precise geographical details. At the time at which it would have existed, the Île de la Cité was made up of four small islets that were often flooded, because they lay at 6 m (20 ft) below sea level. The real location of Lutetia remains a mystery, in spite of the fact that in 2003 the remains of a Gallic *oppidum* were found in Nanterre, with an area of 20 hectares (50 acres) that corresponded to the average size of a main settlement.

The Nanterre *oppidum* consisted of a harbour on the Seine, a commercial centre, districts for different crafts (flour milling, weaving and butchery) and residential areas. Yet Nanterre was called Nemetodurum, not Lutetia, which was 14 km (9 miles) away.

Some archaeologists hold the view that there could have been two *oppida*, one at Nanterre and the other on the Île de la Cité, which complemented each other. Others maintain that Lutetia was situated on an island of the Seine, or on a bank that may have been swallowed up by the river. They believe that there are remaining sites to excavate on the Île de la Cité, which may well have surprises in store.

**ABOVE** Gaulish gold coins which include a stater, a third of a stater and a quarter of a stater. Dating from the first century BC, they were discovered in the riverbed of the Seine, on the Île de la Cité and the Boulevard Saint-Germain. The Parisii used money from c. 100 BC.

**LEFT** Camulogène, the Chief of the Parisii attacks Labienus, Julius Caesar's lieutenant, during the Battle of Lutetia in this painting by Cormon (actually Fernand Anne Piestre, 1845–1924) from 1911.

# Lutetia

Following the Roman conquest, Gaul enjoyed a period of peace and prosperity during the early Roman Empire, from the first until the third century AD. Lutetia became an administrative centre in the historic province of Lyonnais, which had Lyon as its capital. From the third century onwards, Christianity began to develop under the auspices of St Denis, the first Bishop of Paris. St Denis would later be beheaded in the year 250 AD, with his associates on the hill of Montmartre, the name of which means "hill of the martyrs", serving as a reminder of this execution.

The town was split into two sections: the Île de la Cité and St Genevieve's Mount on the Left Bank, away from the flood-prone areas and marshes, although there were also scattered dwellings on the Right Bank. Lutetia was constructed on a grid-plan of streets, radiating from the highest point on St Genevieve's Mount, located at 172–174 rue Saint-Jacques in the 5th arrondissement.

This was the starting point for the main north–south axis, the *cardo maximus* of Lutetia, rue Saint-Jacques. The central road was intersected by secondary roads (*cardines*), which ran parallel to rue Saint-Jacques and crossed it from east to west at right angles (*decumani*), following the standard model of Roman cities.

Lutetia had numerous monuments: a forum (the centre of civic and religious life), three public baths, a theatre and an arena. Two of these monuments, the Cluny baths and the Lutetia arena, have been particularly well preserved. Baths were a fundamental institution in Gallo-Roman civilization, and offered a place for the population to maintain their hygiene and wellbeing through bathing rituals, care of the body, the benefits of physical exercise and the love of sport. They also performed a social function as residents enjoyed meeting up in these places designed for entertainment, relaxation and socializing.

**BELOW** The arena of Lutetia reconstructed in a coloured drawing by Jean-Camille Formigé (1845–1926), 1917. The elliptically-shaped amphitheatre is surrounded by terraces and provides a richly decorated scene.

**RIGHT** Discovered in 1880 in a tomb at 180 Avenue de Choisy (13th arrondissement), this surgeon's set of equipment, dating from c. 275 AD, comprises a number of bronze instruments. Among them are a cauldron, pliers, a spatula, scalpels, probes and buckles that would have been part of the straps used to tie patients down, as well as a box that would have contained various remedies.

**BELOW RIGHT** A clasp in the shape of a boat with three people in it, made out of bronze and dating from the early Roman Empire.

**ABOVE** A view of the great hall of the palace of the thermal baths painted in 1845 by Achille Poirot (1797–after 1852). This was the *frigidarium* of the thermal baths at Cluny, designed for cold baths. The baths are now part of the Musée National du Moyen Age (6 Place Paul-Painlevé, 5th arrondissement), which was formed by the relinking of the baths with the Hôtel de Cluny.

**LEFT** A bronze clasp in the shape of an elephant from the early Roman Empire.

The Cluny baths at 6 Place Paul-Painlevé in the 5th arrondissement – which were built under the rule of Hadrian (117–138 AD), or that of Antonin le Pieux (138–161 AD) – are the only monuments that remain from a far larger complex covering a hectare (two and a half acres). They have been preserved because the building has been constantly repurposed from the Middle Ages, when it became the property of the Cluny monks.

The Lutetia arena at 6 rue des Arènes and 47 rue Monge in the 5th arrondissement used to be an amphitheatre housing one stage. It presented not only gladiator fights and wild beast hunts, but also spectacles involving pantomime, dance or song. Dating from the end of the first century, it was one of the largest in Gaul, measuring 130 m (427 ft) x 100 m (328 ft), and accommodating 17,000 spectators, many more than the 6,000 inhabitants of the town.

During the late Roman Empire, from the fourth until the fifth centuries, the town began to play a major role in the defence plans put in place to deal with Germanic incursions. Emperor Julian the Apostate made Lutetia the headquarters for Roman troops. He could equally well have chosen another town, such as Melun or Soissons, but he was fond of Lutetia, where he was crowned emperor in 360 AD. As he wrote in his book *Misopogon* in 358 AD:

"At that time I was in winter quarters in my beloved Lutetia: this is what the Celts call the small town of the Parisii. It is an islet that lies completely surrounded by the river; wooden bridges lead to it from both sides; the river only seldom ebbs and flows; it stays at more of less the same level in both winter and summer; its water is very pleasant and clear to the eye for those who wish to drink from it. As it is an island, the residents have to draw water from the river... Good vines grow there and some people have taken the trouble to grow fig trees, by wrapping them through winter in either a straw blanket or some other object used to protect the trees from air damage."

During the fourth century, the name Paris – an abbreviation of *civitas Parisiorum* or *urbs Parisiorum*, the town of the Parisii – gained currency over Lutetia. Abandoning the Left Bank, the inhabitants began to withdraw to the Île de la Cité, where two important buildings were erected. On the west side, an imperial palace occupied the spot of the Palais de Justice, at 4 Boulevard du Palais in the 1st arrondissement; and in the east, a basilica stood on the site of Place Louis Lépine in the 4th arrondissement, which might have fulfilled a civic, judicial or military function. The Île de la Cité was turned into a citadel to provide better protection from barbarian raids. It was surrounded by a defensive wall, constructed partly from stone blocks of monuments on the Left Bank. Remains of this rampart can be seen in the crypt of Notre-Dame Cathedral at 7 Parvis Notre-Dame, Place Jean-Paul II in the 4th arrondissement.

**RIGHT** An anthropomorphic bronze vase, dating from the second or third century, which was found at 39–41 rue Pierre Nicole in 1878. The pot, of which only the upper part remains, contained either fragrant powders, such as incense or spices, or perfumed oil.

# The Capital of Clovis's Kingdom

During the dark years of the fifth century, when the Roman Empire was crumbling under the impact of Visigoth, Burgundian, Alemanni and Franconian invaders, three great figures stood out in this rather impenetrable period: St Geneviève, King Clovis and King Childebert I.

Born around 415 ad, Geneviève prophesied in 451 that God would save the town from the Hun invasion. In her capacity as a town magistrate, she wielded her authority over the population, forbidding people to flee and advising women to fast and pray. When Attila, the Hun chieftain, turned away from Paris, Geneviève achieved great acclaim. In recognition of her posterity, she was buried in 502 in a wayside shrine on top of St Geneviève's Mount.

At this shrine, Clovis and his wife Clotilde founded the Basilica of the Apostles, which would later become St Geneviève's Church, their choice for a necropolis. Geneviève was canonized in the eighth century and became the patron saint of Paris. The casket containing her relics, which were worshipped in the Abbey of St Geneviève, were carried through the city in a procession during times of crisis, such as the catastrophic floods of 1496.

The abbey, which was renowned for its intellectual influence, was demolished in 1790 and its church, that of St Geneviève, was then converted into the Pantheon, whereas its monastic buildings were turned into the Lycée Henri IV in 1796. Today the cloister, stairway of the prophets, library, chapel, kitchens, refectory and bell tower are lasting reminders of the lost abbey.

Clovis (466–511), the king of one of the Salian Frankish tribes, successfully fought the Roman army at the Battle of Soissons in 486 and expanded his dominion as far as the Loire. Queen Clotilde and Geneviève urged him to convert to the Catholic faith. But Clovis mirrored Emperor Constantine by renouncing paganism to embrace Christianity after his hard-fought victory over the Alemanni at Tolbiac in 496. Clovis was baptized by the Bishop of Reims (St Remigius), in the company of 3,000 Frankish warriors, on a date that remains unclear – 25 December in either 497, 498, or 499.

This conversion to Christianity sealed the alliance between civil power and religious authority, allowing for the merger of the Franks and the Gallo-Romans, which led to a flowering of great religious buildings. The roots of the French monarchy's divine right to rule lie in this founding baptism. In 508, Clovis established the seat of his kingdom in the former palace of the Roman emperors, making Paris his preferred place of residence. As a result, Paris attained the rank of capital city, a status that it maintained until the seventh century.

**LEFT** The Tower of Clovis, the old bell tower of the Abbey of Saint Geneviève, situated in the Lycée Henri IV.

**OPPOSITE** Showing a votive offering by the City of Paris to Sainte Geneviève, this painting by Georges Lallemant and Philippe de Champaigne (dated c. 1625) is from the Church of Montigny-Lencoup, Seinte-et-Marne. The Provost-Marshal of the merchants and the aldermen offered this picture to the Abbey of Sainte Geneviève to commemorate the procession which took place on 26 July 1625 in order to disperse the torential rains: the saint, holding a candle and the keys of Paris drifts above a view of the capital where one can see the Left Bank and the hill of Montmartre.

King Childebert I (511–558), Clovis's son, oversaw the construction of St Étienne's Cathedral, the outline of which is recreated on the square in front of Notre-Dame Cathedral. In 558, he founded the Basilica of Sainte-Croix and Saint-Vincent (now the Church of Saint-Germain-des-Prés), as a shrine for the precious relics brought back from Spain – the tunic of Saint Vincent and a golden cross of Toledo containing a fragment of the true Cross. Childebert planned to turn this basilica into a royal necropolis adjoining the abbey, and lavished it with substantial funds. In the sanctuary, consecrated on 23 December 558, Childebert was buried in a sarcophagus laid in a hollowed-out grave beneath the church paving, following a funereal custom inaugurated by Clovis. Rich and powerful, the abbey became renowned for its school of illuminators, who illustrated ancient texts, and for the scholarly works written by its historians. The abbey was destroyed in 1790, except for the Church of Saint-Germain-des-Prés and the abbatial palace.

In the sixth and seventh centuries, Merovingian kings preferred to live in the country palaces of Reuil and Clichy, which weakened the standing of Paris. However, this period of relative peace favoured the reoccupation of the Left Bank by about 12 churches, such as Saint-Séverin and Saint-Marcel. Meanwhile, on the Right Bank, the population congregated around the Churches of Saint-Paul-des-Champs, Saint-Gervais and Saint-Martin-des-Champs, as evidenced by the household objects and weapons dug up during excavations carried out near these buildings.

Throughout the ninth century, Scandinavians took to their longboats and surged into Paris in successive waves, pillaging the monasteries' treasures, sacking the city, burning houses and churches, stealing jewels, money, vessels, cult objects, *pallia frisonica* cloth, Frankish swords and other light portable spoils. They captured slaves and held rulers to ransom on several occasions. The terrified populace took refuge on the Île de la Cité, the perimeter wall of which was buttressed. To strengthen the island's defences, King Charles the Bald constructed the bridge bearing his name on the site of Pont-au-Change in 870, a proper barrage flanked by a fortified tower and in 885, he added a defensive tower at the Petit-Pont entrance.

In November 885, a Viking army of 700 vessels and 40,000 men, reputed to be invincible, laid siege to Paris for more than a year. Entrenched in the Île de la Cité, the population put up a brave resistance, spurred on by Bishop Gozlin. In the end Odo, Count of Paris, negotiated a financial deal to get rid of the enemy, whose murderous raids took the city into a period of decline that lasted until the eleventh century.

# The Accession of the Capetians

The hero of the Paris siege, Count Odo, ruled the Duchy of France from 888 until 898. His great nephew, Hugues Capet, elected king by his peers in 987, founded the Capetian dynasty, which would reign in a direct line of succession to the throne until 1328. The administrative centre was established in the Palais de la Cité, which was restored by Robert the Pious (996–1031), whereas the Treasury was entrusted to the Knights Templar. Louis VI (1108–1137) and Louis VII (1137–1180) settled in Paris at a time when the city was experiencing substantial demographic expansion. This royal patronage stimulated the city's economic, religious and artistic renaissance.

Economic activity was concentrated around the Place and Port de Grève (now Place de l'Hôtel de Ville), where the natural cove proved propitious for commerce on the river. Situated near Le Châtelet – the headquarters of the Paris provost and the butchers' quarter – the site benefited from its proximity to a busy crossroads and offered direct access to the Île de la Cité via the Grand-Pont, which was built in 1142. Gold and silversmiths and money-changers set up shop here, giving the construction its name of Pont-au-Change.

Porters unloaded wine from Burgundy, wheat from La Beauce, logs and timber, and freestones on the jetties of Port de Grève. Boats drew up alongside the Port de l'Ecole (Quai du Louvre) and sailed up the Seine, loaded with fish, wood, salt, Normandy cider and wine from Meudon. The "water merchants" who controlled these transactions formed a wealthy guild called the Hanseatic League, which was approved by Louis VI in 1134. Not far from the warehouses, the king set up the market at Les Champeaux in 1137, the beginnings of what would become Les Halles, which gradually developed into the economic heart of the city.

Flourishing districts emerged around churches such as Saint-Gervais and Saint-Germain-l'Auxerrois. The Priory of Saint-Martin-des-Champs, built in 1067, and the enclosure of the Temple fortress, established around 1150, also created significant hubs of expansion in the city. Louis VI and Adélaïde of Savoy founded the Abbey of Montmartre in 1134; its church, Saint-Pierre, consecrated in 1147, still stands at the top of the Butte of Montmartre.

Whereas the Right Bank grew northwards, the Left Bank developed more slowly, because it took 150 years to restore abbeys such as Saint-Marcel, which had been destroyed by Norman raids. The Abbey of Saint-Victor, famous for its scholarly teachings, was recognized by Pope Innocent III in 1160. Construction began at this time on the Church of Saint-Julien le Pauvre, a rare example of Roman art in Paris. The Abbey of Saint-Germain-des-Prés led to the expansion of the Saint-Germain borough, where a famous annual fair was established in 1176.

**RIGHT** The coronation sword and scabbard of the kings of France, known as "Joyeuse" ("Joyful") or the Sword of Charlemagne. The top of the hilt dates from the tenth or eleventh century; the hilt from the twelfth century and the blade from the thirteenth. Made of gold and steel and decorated with seed pearls, silver gilt, cabuchons, precious stones and embroidered velvet, the scabbard is embroidered with fleurs de lys and was created for the coronation of Charles X in 1825.

*[Illuminated manuscript in medieval Latin script]*

**RIGHT** The chevet (polygonal east end) of the Church of Saint-Pierre de Montmartre, 2 rue de Mont-Cenis (18th arrondissement). Even though it has been restored, the church has kept the characteristics of Roman art in its layout and chevet, which dates from 1180.

**RIGHT** A decorated fan box with a view of Les Halles showing the merchants offering fish for sale. It was painted in gouache by an anonymous artist c. 1680.

The Bishop of Paris, Maurice de Sully, demolished the Church of Saint-Étienne in order to reorganize the religious life of La Cité: Notre-Dame Cathedral opened out on to a square with a fountain, its boundaries set by a low wall, facilitating access via a 3m (10 ft) wide road, geared to suit processions of the faithful. The new Episcopal Palace and Hôtel-Dieu were constructed between 1163 and 1330 in the adjoining space to the Gothic cathedral.

This massive edifice – 127 m (416 ft) long, 40 m (130 ft) wide and 33m (108 ft) high under the vaults – is made up of a ten-bay nave and a choir with double ambulatory. Famous artists worked on the construction, such as Jean de Chelles (architect of the transept arms and the choir chapels), Pierre de Montreuil (who designed the

rose windows and statuary) and Jean Le Bouteillier (who sculpted the jube and stone screen). However, in the seventeenth and eighteenth centuries, the harmonious balance of this masterpiece of Gothic art was ruined, and the structure was vandalized during the French Revolution.

From 1845 until 1864, Eugène Viollet-le-Duc directed a huge restoration project, reinstating the spire, gables, pinnacles and sculptures on the west and south façades. Now, about 30,000 visitors and pilgrims come to Notre-Dame Cathedral every day to admire the chevet, with its trademark flying buttresses; portal sculptures, choir, vaults and great organ; and paintings, stained-glass windows and treasury.

# THE ABBEY OF SAINT-DENIS

As the story goes, Denis was beheaded about 250 AD and buried in the north of Paris, where Geneviève built a chapel. Dagobert brought the saint's coffin to the Abbey of Saint-Denis, which Capetian kings later adopted as the official necropolis. Abbot Suger, a minister under Louis VI, lavished the abbey with sumptuous gifts and developed the ceremony of the royal coronation. On this day, the regalia comprising the insignia of knighthood (spurs and sword), royal crown and cloak, sceptre (Hand of Justice) and liturgical instruments, which were kept in the abbey, were all taken to Reims Cathedral. They are now on display in the Louvre museum, alongside rare items from the Treasury of Saint-Denis.

**RIGHT** An extract from the 1317 illuminated manuscript of *La Vie de Monseigneur Saint-Denis* (*The Life of Monsignor Saint Denis*) by a monk known as Yves. In the top part Saint Denis confers on Saint Antonin the duty of writing the story of his life, while below, scenes of everyday life unfold on the Grand Pont (Great Bridge): a chariot passes by; a passer-by visits a shop while boats laden with goods and people in the middle of tasting and selling wine move along the Seine.

**OVERLEAF LEFT** An interior view of Notre-Dame Cathedral in 1789 painted by J-F Despelchin. The cathedral was completed in the fourteenth century. The nave, with its ribbed and vaulted ceiling is decorated with 76 large pictures, known as "les Mays", which were offered to the cathedral by the members of the Company of Tradesmen in 1707. This exceptional collection has since been broken up.

**OVERLEAF RIGHT** The west façade of the Cathedral of Nôtre-Dame in Paris, which ws built on the Île de la Cité between the twelfth and fourteenth centuries.

# The Influence of Philippe Auguste

Concerned about public health, Philippe Auguste (1180–1223) paved the main thoroughfares, which were swimming in mud, and closed the Cemetery of the Innocents. In 1190, the king ordered that Paris should be protected by a 6–8-m (20–26-ft) high rampart, topped by a covered way and flanked by towers reserved for crossbowmen. This solid-stone wall was known as Philippe Auguste's *enceinte* (inner ring of fortifications) and punctuated by 12 gates along the busiest roads. This defensive structure was built on the Right Bank from 1190 until 1209, and on the Left Bank between 1200 and 1215.

In an outpost to the west, beside the Seine, the king constructed a square castle in 1204, a precursor of the Louvre. He deposited the treasury and archives in the 30-m (100-ft) high central donjon, called the Great Tower. The plinth of the donjon and its ditch, which were uncovered in 1983 when the square courtyard of the Louvre palace was being excavated, are the outstanding remains of this medieval fortress.

The perimeter of the *enceinte*, which excluded the boroughs that had sprung up around the Abbeys of Saint-Victor, Saint-Germain-des-Prés, Saint-Marcel and Saint-Martin-des-Champs, enclosed an

**LEFT** A depiction of Philippe le Bel (Philip the Good) and his family from the 1313 manuscript of the *Book of Kalila va dimna* (translated by Raymond de Béziers). The king, centre, is surrounded by the future King Louis X (wearing the crown) and Isabelle, the wife of King Edward II of England. Also present are the future King Charles IV and King Philippe V.

**BELOW** The remains of the *enceinte* (wall) of Philippe-Auguste, which can be seen at 5–21 rue des Jardins Saint-Paul (4th arrondissement). The wall which is 120 m (394 ft) long and 6–7 m (19¾–23 ft) tall has lost its parapet which would have increased its height to 8–9 m (26¼–29½ ft). Behind it, one can see the chevet of the Church of Saint-Paul-Saint-Louis.

**OPPOSITE** Remains of the dungeons and moats of Philippe-Auguste's Louvre, which can be found in the basement of the Louvre Museum's courtyard.

# LA SAINTE-CHAPELLE

St Louis acquired relics of the Passion that he wanted to exhibit in a prestigious monument, possibly constructed by Pierre de Montreuil. This building, which is conspicuous because of its unusual height of 43 m (140 ft), has an upper chapel that was formerly reserved for the worship of the relics. It is illuminated by 14 huge stained-glass windows supported by fine stone columns with exquisitely carved capitals depicting a varied range of types of foliage (thistles, oak, fig and holly), flowers, birds and people. The chapel is famous for its representation of subjects derived from the Old and New Testaments, and for its beautiful stained-glass windows, which suffuse it in a stunning red and blue light.

**OPPOSITE** The Palace of the City and the Sainte Chapelle, a miniature by the Limbourg Brothers from the *Très riches heures du duc de Berry, le mois de juin*, c. 1416. The buildings and gardens then occupied a quadrilateral area of about 110 x 135 m (361 x 443 ft) enclosed by walls.

**ABOVE** The execution of the Templiers from Boccaccio's *De Casibus* (translated by Laurent de Premierfait), from the fifteenth century. Legend has it that at his torture Jacques de Molay placed a curse on the king: "You will all be cursed unto the thirteenth generation of your family." Philippe le Bel died within the year, some months after Pope Clement V.

**RIGHT** Louis XV, aged five, emerges from the Grand Chamber of Parliament where he had been proclaimed king. He is shown in the "Cour de Mai", which is accurately portrayed in this gouache by Denis Martin le Jeune from 1715, where one can see the Sainte Chapelle in the centre, the Cour des Comptes on the left and the Chapel of Saint-Michel on the right.

area of 253 hectares (625 acres) and established a new framework for urban development. The inner city was divided into three sections – the Right Bank was called "la Ville", the Left Bank was known as "l'Université" and the island was described as "la Cité" – and then subdivided into 33 parishes. By the end of the thirteenth century, about 80,000 inhabitants occupied this area.

On the Left Bank the teaching provided by the Church dominated all other activities. Carried out in the early twelfth century in the canonical school of Notre-Dame, it flourished under the teachers of the Abbeys of Saint Geneviève and Saint Victor, who gave lessons in barns or in the open air around Place Maubert. In 1200, Philippe Auguste granted special jurisdiction to the university, which became an autonomous body under the control of the Pope. Its great reputation attracted students from England, Germany, Sweden, Normandy and Picardy, who came to study the arts, law, medicine and theology. They were lodged in colleges, the most famous of which, the Sorbonne, was created in 1257 by Robert de Sorbon. The students spoke Latin, resulting in the christening of Saint Geneviève's Mount as "the Latin Quarter".

In the early thirteenth century, the mendicant orders – Cordeliers, Augustinians, Jacobins, Carmelites, Dominicans and Carthusians – established themselves in Paris. The monks provided places for lodging and teaching, as well as spacious churches, so they controlled extensive property assets. Similarly, the Order of the Knights Templar, established on a fortified plot of land measuring six hectares (15 acres), wielded considerable power in terms of land and finance.

The palace on La Cité increased in scope under the reign of Louis IX (Saint Louis, 1214–1270), who ordered the construction of the Treasury of Charters for the archive deposit, as well as Sainte-Chapelle, the jewel of Gothic art consecrated in 1248. In 1299, Philippe IV (the Fair, 1296–1313) had begun to reorganize the palace to accommodate the main government bodies and the realm's administrative staff, and he set up the Conciergerie. The concierge was a kind of steward, who was responsible for controlling the supplies that came into the palace; he also dispensed justice, imprisoning people in jails set up in the towers. The dungeon supervisors were based in the Guard Room. The Hall of the Men-at-Arms was built in 1312 and served as a refectory for the 3,000 guards and palace officials. The parliament of Paris, the first supreme court of justice in the kingdom, met in the Great Hall.

Philippe the Fair wanted to create a centralized modern state, but the military orders such as the Knights Templar – exempt from taxes and under the authority of Pope Clement V – posed an obstacle to this policy. Around 1306, the king instructed the Knights Templar to merge with the Knights of St John of Jerusalem in order to finance a crusade that he would lead. However, the Grand Master of the Order, Jacques de Molay, refused and the Templars were arrested in 1307, their possessions confiscated. Cruelly tortured and accused of heresy in an unfair trial, 50 Templars were burned at the stake in 1314.

**RIGHT** Braun's map (dated 1572) of Paris circa 1530 is oriented to the east. The Right Bank is enclosed by Charles V's *enceinte* (defensive wall). It is still possible to make out the traces of Philippe Auguste's *enceinte*, surrounded by building works: it continued to protect the Left Bank and was strengthened in the fifteenth century.

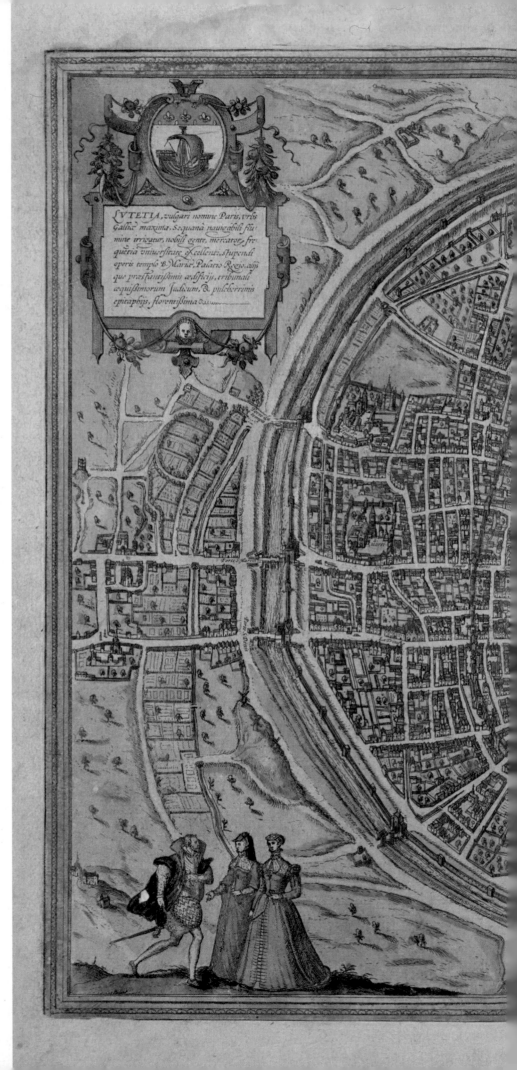

La Aubou
La Tour de billy
S. Ladre S. Marcel
S. Clare

Riviere de Saine

La Tour de Nella
La Tour de vege

PARIS pour vray eft la maiſõ roÿalle,    Jnde en eſtude, & en poetes Romme,    Fecunde en vin, doulce en ſes Citoÿens.
Du dieu Phœbus en ſplendeur radiale    Athenes lors en diét treſſcauãt homme,    Fertile en bled, & en maintz diuſeres
Ceſt Cerrhea pleine de bons eſpritz.    Rozier mondain, baulme du firmament,    biens.
Treſuigoureux faiſans diuers eſcriptz.    Vniuerſel, de Sidon ſomment    
Ceſt Chryſea en metaulx habondante    Tres habondante en viures et breuuciges,    
Grece de pris en liures floriſſante    Riche en beaulx champs & fluueuZ riuages    Cum Priuilegio

# The Middle Ages

During the Hundred Years War, the French and English battled for control of the kingdom of France from 1337 until 1453. After his defeat at Poitiers in 1356, King Jean II (known as "the Good" [1319–1364]) was taken prisoner and held captive in England for three years. His son – the Dauphin and later Charles V (1338–1380) – reigned as regent during this time.

Famines and epidemics exacted a terrible toll. The Great Plague, or Black Death, originated in the Black Sea and was transmitted via shipping routes to Provence. The disease had reached Paris by 1348, where it wiped out a significant part of the population.

In 1357, Étienne Marcel – the provost of merchants from 1355 until 1358 and the capital's most senior magistrate – bought the Maison aux Piliers on Place de Grève (now Place de l'Hôtel de Ville), which was the hub of economic life, and turned it into the city's administrative headquarters. Since then, municipal power has rested firmly on this spot.

By 1358, Marcel and the Paris bourgeoisie were attempting to exercise control over the monarchy. On 22 February 1358, the provost and rioters invaded the Palais de la Cité. Two advisors to Charles V – the Marshall of Champagne Jean de Conflans and the Marshall of Normandy Robert de Clermont – were killed in the struggle.

The uprising led Charles V to leave the palace and set up a new royal residence on the Right Bank in 1361: Hôtel Saint-Pol, near to rue Saint-Paul in the 4th arrondissement, an amalgamation of several aristocratic and ecclesiastical homes.

Charles V was a great builder. In 1364, he entrusted the refurbishment of the Louvre to the architect Raymond du Temple, who transformed it into a pleasant residence with a large garden. Security in the capital presented a major challenge due to the English threat. Paris was no longer protected by Philippe Auguste's fortifications, which had become rundown and surrounded by homes. Moreover, they had not been adapted to prepare the city for the arrival of artillery and cannon fire. From 1356 until 1358, Marcel had ditches dug out as a matter of urgency to improve the city's defences. Continuing these works, Charles V built a new *enceinte* on the Right Bank in 1365, which was completed in 1420 during the reign of Charles VI. On the Left Bank, Charles V reinforced the *enceinte* constructed by Philippe Auguste with ditches.

Charles V's *enceinte*, punctuated by six gates, followed the route of the present Grands Boulevards. It was reinforced by fortifications known as *bastides* or *bastilles*. On 22 April 1370, Hugues Aubriot, the provost of Paris, laid the first stone of the Bastille Saint-Antoine, which would become as famous as La Bastille. Situated at the eastern end of rue Saint-Antoine, it offered protection for Hôtel Saint-Pol.

This was the favourite townhouse of Charles VI (1368–1422), who suffered from fits of madness after 1392. On 28 January 1393, it hosted the wedding celebrations of a lady-in-waiting of

**ABOVE** The assassination of Etienne Marcel on 31 July 1358 by supporters of King Charles V at the gate of Saint-Antoine (8–11 rue de la Bastille) depicted in an illumination by Jean Froissart, from *Chronicles*, dating from the fifteenth century. The gate was the only entrance on the east side of the capital and adjoined the Bastille.

**LEFT** The vault of the grand staircase in the Tower of Jean sans Peur at 20 rue Etienne-Marcel (2nd arrondissement). The tower dates from 1409 to 1411 and is the only remains of the Hôtel de Jean sans Peur, the Duke of Burgundy. It is decorated with superb carvings representing branches and leaves of oak, hops and hawthorn.

**OPPOSITE** The month of October, a miniature by the Limbourg Brothers and Barthélemy d'Eyck from *Les très riches heures de Jean de Berry*, c. 1411–15. Behind the Seine and the high wall is the Louvre Palace.

RIGHT One of the aisles of the Church of Saint-Séverin, 1 rue des Prêtres Saint-Séverin in the 5th arrondissement. The double aisle of the church is supported by pillars comprising multiple strands which form a star-shaped palm of stone.

Queen Isabeau of Bavaria, Charles VI's wife. The king and five lords dressed up as wild men to mark the occasion. But a torch accidentally set fire to the men's costumes, burning four of them alive. The Duchess of Berry saved the monarch by covering him with the cloth of her long train. This tragic party became known as the "*Bal des Ardents*" (Ball of the Burning Men). After the death of Charles VI in 1422, the Louvre was no longer used as a royal residence, and acted as a prison and arsenal instead.

France was embroiled in war on 6 March 1429 when Joan of Arc (1412–31), the daughter of well-to-do farmers from Domrémy in Vosges, went to see the king, Charles VII, who had fled to Chinon. Leading a detachment of soldiers granted to her by the king, she managed to save Orléans from the English on 29 April 1429. After deciding to attack Paris, she was defeated and wounded on 8 September 1429 in front of Porte Saint-Honoré at 161–167 rue Saint-Honoré in the 1st arrondissement. The French recaptured the city from the English in 1436 and on 12 November 1437, Charles VII made his solemn entrance into the capital.

In the second half of the fifteenth century, Paris gradually became a safe city again. Kings Charles VIII and Louis XII preferred to reside on the banks of the Loire, whereas the Parliament and Chamber of Accounts (financial court), were established in Paris. Princes and prelates built sumptuous homes in a flamboyant Gothic style, such as the Paris residence of the Dukes of Burgundy, which was extended for Jean the Fearless (Duke of Burgundy from 1404 until 1419) by the architect Pierre de Hebuterne. However, only the tower still stands, at 20 rue Étienne-Marcel in the 2nd arrondissement.  In the Latin Quarter, Jacques d'Amboise, Abbot of Cluny from 1485 until 1510, built the Hôtel de Cluny at 6 Place Paul-Painlevé in the 5th arrondissement, beside the ancient thermal baths. In the Marais district, Tristan de Salazar, Archbishop of Sens, constructed the Hôtel de Sens between 1498 and 1507 at 1 rue du Figuier in the 4th arrondissement for the Archbishops of Sens, who were also Bishops of Paris until 1622. The Flamboyant Gothic style reached its peak in the church of Saint-Séverin and the old churches were restored.

RIGHT  The Hôtel de Cluny in 1850, painted by Achille Poirot (1797– after 1852). The State acquired the Hôtel de Cluny in 1843 to house its mediaeval and renaissance collections assembled by Alexandre du Sommerard. It became the Musée National du Moyen Age (6 Place Paul-Painlevé, 5th arrondissement) and includes the thermal baths.

BELOW  A seventeenth-century engraving by Jacques Rigaud of the Bastille, the Saint-Antoine Gate and part of the faubourg. The Bastille, which was only 24 m (78¾ ft) high, comprised eight towers and was re-enforced during the reign of Henri II by a bastion.

# Growth in the Sixteenth Century

**D**uring the Renaissance, Paris emerged as a flourishing city. Its growth was linked to the decision of Kings François I and Henri II to live in the capital: in 1528, François I (1494–1547) established his residence in the Louvre palace, where he razed the keep to the ground. In 1546, he entrusted the refurbishment of the Louvre to Pierre Lescot, who completed the Renaissance masterpiece, the Lescot Wing, under the reign of Henri II.

Following the example of the Italian cities he had admired during the wars in Italy, François I decided in 1533 that Paris should have a magnificent Hôtel de Ville to replace the dilapidated "house on pillars". The Italian architect Dominique de Cortone undertook the construction of the monument. However, this building process was interrupted by religious wars, so it was continued by the architects Marin de la Vallée, then Pierre II Chambiges, Claude Guillain and Claude Vellefaux until 1628.

The capital became more densely populated after royal and private land was parcelled into lots. François I tried to finance the expenditure caused by wars, his château building, the sumptuous court life and his policy of patronage. To this end he sold uninhabited royal properties in 1543, such as the townhouses of the Counts of Flanders and Tancarville. Hôtel Saint-Pol, abandoned since the reign of Charles VII, was given over to a parcel of lots, based on roads laid out around 1544. These included rue Charles V and rue des Lions-Saint-Paul, conjuring up the menagerie in Hôtel Saint-Pol; rue de la Cerisaie, evoking the cherry trees in the townhouse's gardens; and rue Beautreillis, recalling the garden trellisses when it was built around 1555.

**ABOVE** King François I of France, c. 1530–35, in a painting from the studio of Joos van Clève (c. 1485–1540).

**LEFT** The Place de Grève and the Hôtel de Ville during a public festival, around 1640, in a painting from the Flemish School. The Hôtel de Ville was completed in the seventeenth century and is seen still surrounded by mediaeval houses which would be knocked down when the building was enlarged during the reign of Louis-Philippe. The Hôtel de Ville was destroyed during the Commune of 1871.

**OPPOSITE** The courtyard of the Hôtel Carnavalet (23 rue de Sévigné, 3rd arrondiseement). Built for Jacques des Ligneris, the President of the Parlement de Paris, in 1548–60, since 1880 it has been dedicated as the Musée Carnavalet to the history of Paris.

PARIS

**PREVIOUS PAGES** The market and the fountain of the Innocents in a painting from 1822 by John-James Chalon (1778–1854). The fountain was erected at the corner of rue Saint-Denis and rue Berger by Pierre Lescot (c. 1515–78) and Jean Goujon (c. 1510–c. 1565) to commemorate the entry into Paris by Henri II on 16 June 1549. Moved in the eighteenth century to the Market of the Innocents, it was transformed into a square shape of which the fourth side was sculpted in 1788 by Augustin Pajou (1730–1809). Another modification in 1858 saw the fountain moved to Place Joachim du Bellay in the 1st arrondissement.

The Marais quarter held great appeal for the nobility, as seen in the successful lot parcelling of the Culture Sainte-Catherine. When they found themselves in financial difficulties, the members of Sainte-Catherine du Val des Ecoliers priory, at Place Saint-Catherine in the 4th arrondissement, divided their cultivated land into suitable building plots and put it up for sale in 1545. Seven private townhouses in these lots have survived, marked out by rue des Francs-Bourgeois, rue de Sévigné, rue Payenne, rue Elzévir, rue du Parc Royal and rue Pavée: they are the Hôtel Carnavalet (now Musée Carnavalet), Hôtel de Lamoignon (now the Bibliothèque Historique de la Ville de Paris), Hôtel de Donon (now Musée Cognacq-Jay), Hôtel de Marle (now the Swedish Cultural Centre), as well as the Hôtel de Savourny, Hôtel de Châtillon and Hôtel d'Albret.

From 1553 Henri II (1519–59), François I's son, reinforced the *enceinte* built by Charles V, adding bastions to keep pace with artillery developments. In 1550, the king undertook the modernization of Les Halles market, continuing these works until 1560. In 1559, Henri II negotiated a peace treaty with Spain, which was sealed by the marriages of his daughter Élisabeth of France to King Philippe II of Spain, and her sister Marguerite de Valois to Emmanuel-Philibert of Savoy. During the wedding celebrations, Henri II took part in a joust against Gabriel de Montgomery, the captain of the Scottish guard, who wounded him by accident. The king was taken to the royal residence Hôtel des Tournelles, on Place des Vosges in the 3rd and 4th arrondissements, where he died on 10 July 1559.

Overcome by grief at the loss, his widow Catherine de' Medici had this townhouse knocked down in 1564, because it was full of sad memories. Catherine erected the Tuileries Palace near to

**ABOVE** The massacre of Saint-Barthélémy depicted in an engraving from the sixteenth century. It began on 24 August 1772, the day of Saint-Barthélémy, and continued until 29 August.

**RIGHT** The ball given on 24 September 1581 at the court of Henri III for the marriage of Anne, the Duke of Joyeuse, a favourite of Henri III, and Marguerite de Vaudémont-Lorraine. In this anonymous painting from the end of the sixteenth century the married couple are performing a dance in a room in the Lescot Wing of the Louvre Palace. Henri III is sitting on a daïs on the left with his mother, Catherine de' Medici.

the Louvre, assigning the project to the architect Philibert de l'Orme in 1564, and following his death in 1570, to Jean Bullant. The three sons of Henri II and Catherine de' Medici – François II (1544–60), Charles IX (1550–74) and Henri III (1551–89) – all became kings of France. Catherine de' Medici acted as regent during the brief reign of François II, aged 15 when he was crowned king, and at the start of the reign of Charles IX, who succeeded his brother at the age of ten.

Wars of religion broke out during this turbulent period. On 18 August 1572, Marguerite de Valois (sister of Charles IX) and the Protestant King Henri de Navarre (the future Henri IV) were married in Notre-Dame Cathedral. Catherine de' Medici succeeded

in persuading Charles IX to eliminate the Protestant leaders, who had come to the capital for the ceremony. The Saint Bartholomew's Day Massacre was carried out during 24–29 August 1572, when Admiral de Coligny and members of the Protestant community, numbering several thousand, were killed and had their homes ransacked.

Two years later, Henri III was crowned king. In 1588, he passed a law stating that the 16 administrative districts of Paris should be named after their main church, such as Quartier Notre-Dame and Quartier du Temple. On 1 August 1589, the king was stabbed at Saint-Cloud by the monk Jacques Clément: on his deathbed, he named Henri de Navarre as his heir.

# Henri IV

Henri de Bourbon, (son of Antoine de Bourbon, Duke of Vendôme, and Jeanne d'Albret, Queen of Navarre) was the great nephew of François I by virtue of his birth in 1553, and, through his marriage to Marguerite de Valois, the brother-in-law of Henri III, who died in 1589 without an heir. In accordance with Salic law, Henri de Navarre (as he was also known) became the legitimate heir to the French throne. However, as Catholics would not tolerate a Protestant king, they refused to recognize this succession and rebelled. Henri de Navarre tried to retake the kingdom by force, with the result being that the religious war also became a civil conflict. In 1590, the King of Navarre laid siege to Paris without success. After renouncing his Calvinist faith in the Basilica of Saint-Denis in 1593, he was crowned king under the name of Henri IV on 27 February 1594 in Chartres Cathedral. His entry into the capital on 22 March 1594 restored civil peace after 30 years of fighting. On 30 April 1598, the king signed the Edict of Nantes, which allowed the Protestant faith to be practised in appropriate places. After the annulment of his first marriage, the king married Marie de' Medici in 1601, the daughter of the Grand Duke of Tuscany.

**BELOW** Painted by Peter Paul Rubens, Henri IV is shown leaving for the war against Germany and conferring the government of the kingdom upon his wife on 20 March 1610. The work is part of a cycle known as *The Life of Marie de' Medici* made for the Luxembourg Palace.

**RIGHT** The Hospital of Saint-Louis, situated between the Faubourgs of Montmartre and Saint-Laurent, is shown in an etching by Jean Mariette from the end of the seventeenth century.

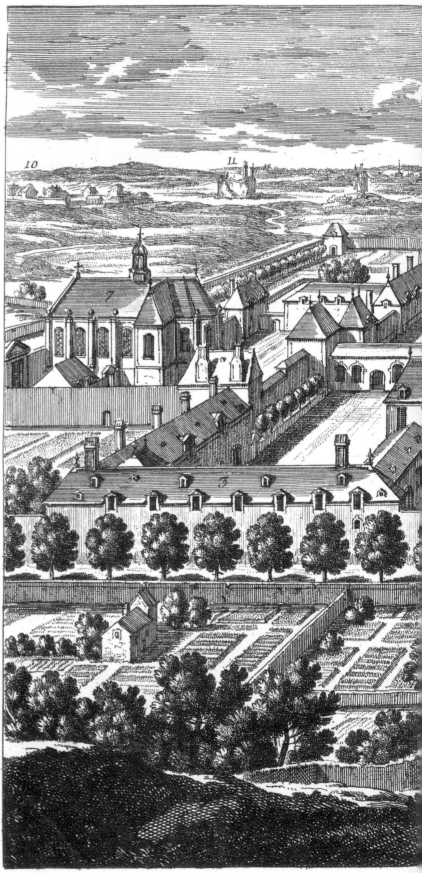

The king restored the country's economy, supporting the arts and industry, and in 1607 he established the Hôpital Saint-Louis, displaying his passion for architecture. In 1595, he conceived the Grand Plan for the Louvre and saw the completion of its first stage: joining up the Louvre and the Tuileries Palace with a 450-m (1,475-ft) long corridor – the Waterside Gallery, or Grande Galerie – built by Jacques II Androuet du Cerceau and Louis Métezeau.

In 1601, his interest in developments in the textile industry led him to assign the monopoly for tapestry-making "in the Flanders style" to two Flemish craftsmen running a workshop – the birthplace of the Gobelin manufacturers. As he wished to develop

the silk industry, he planted mulberry trees and invited Milanese artisans to teach silk weaving in a factory he set up on the site of the Palais des Tournelles. In 1605, his minister Maximilien de Béthune, Duke of Sully, knocked it down in order to turn the site into a residential square, now Place des Vosges.

The square is lined with 34 identical pavilions in brick and stone, with shops facing on to an arcade. The Pavilions of the King and Queen form two monumental entrances to Place Royale, which was inaugurated by a memorable event: the double wedding of Louis XIII to Anne of Austria and Elisabeth of France to the future Philippe IV of Spain. During 5–7 April 1612, festivities took place,

including military parades, hoop races, songs, spectacles, fireworks and a carousel.

At the tip of the Île de la Cité, Henri IV developed a splendid city-plan: in 1607 he completed the Pont-Neuf (initiated by Henri III) and created the Place Dauphine. Measuring 238 m (780 ft) long by 20 m (65 ft) wide, Pont-Neuf was the first bridge to cross the Seine without interruption. A cornice decorated with 381 mascarons sits on top of its 12 stone arches, which rest on piers crowned with half moons. These bearded satyrs, wearing diadems of shells and grape bunches, were sculpted by Germain Pilon and re-created in the nineteenth century.

**ABOVE** The Pont-Neuf, seen from the entrance to the Place Dauphine, and the Collège de Quatre-Nations and the Louvre, c. 1666, in a French School painting from the seventeenth century. The equestrian statue of Henri IV, commissioned by Jean de Boulogne, stands in the middle of the bridge against the backdrop of the quay of the Louvre Palace looking towards the west of the capital. It was the first effigy of a royal person to be erected in a public place.

**LEFT** An engraving entitled *L'Hiver* (*Winter*) by Abraham Bosse. At the beginning of the seventeenth century the east bedroom was the favourite room in an apartment. In this room full of tapestries, a group of companions warm themselves in front of the fire, toasting beignets, an allusion to Shrove Tuesday.

**BELOW** The prison register of the Conciergerie, recording the admission into this prison of François Ravaillac on 16 May 1610, and the summary of his sentence.

**OPPOSITE** The assassination of Henri IV by Ravaillac on 14 May 1610. The king was stabbed in his carriage which was held up by a traffic jam in the rue de la Ferronnerie in the 1st arrondissement.

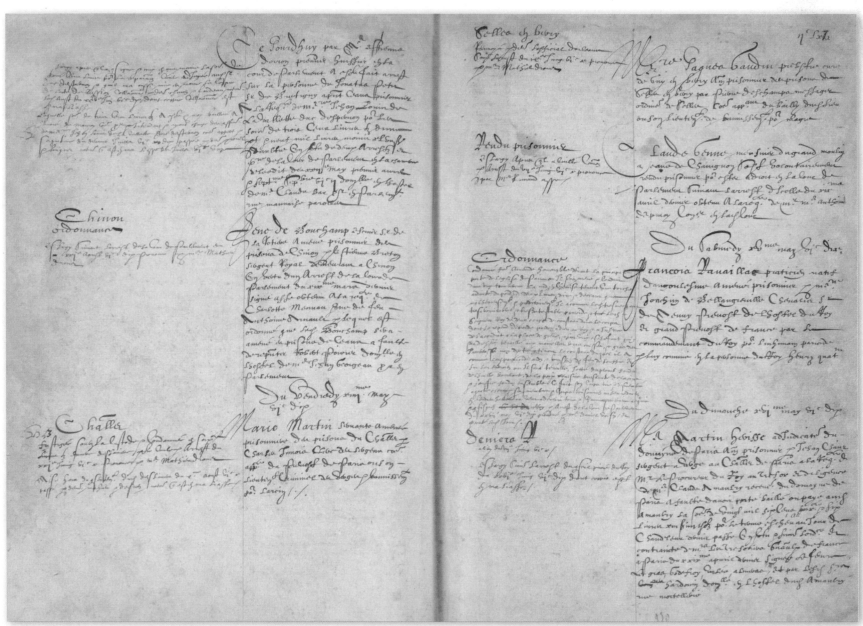

In its openness to traffic and departure from the tradition of bridges lined with houses, the structure was deemed to be revolutionary and became hugely popular. Stalls selling sweetmeats or books were set up on the pavements. Hawkers, shoe blacks, dog clippers and men renting out parasols shared the space with the statue of Henri IV, erected in 1614. Girls selling flowers, oranges and coconuts joined hucksters and actors in shouting at passers-by.

To make the best use of the triangular point of the Île de la Cité, which had been dug out artificially, Henri IV devised the Place Dauphine, a closed space devoted to commerce. Between 1608 and 1616, the master stonemason François Petit built 44 identical houses, each with three floors and a shopfront. The brick and stone façades and slate roofs produced a colourful and well-balanced ensemble, which was further emphasized by the two pavilions situated at the entrance to the bridge. The continuation of the bridge was punctuated by the rue Dauphine, which was 10 m (32 ft) wide – an exceptional size for that time – in order to attract the population to the Left Bank, inside Philippe Auguste's *enceinte*.

On 14 May 1610, the day after the queen's coronation, Henri IV set off for the Arsenal, the residence of the Duke of Sully. Even though he had escaped about 15 assassination attempts, this time the king succumbed to the dagger of François Ravaillac. Historians have not been able to clarify whether this regicide was the act of an isolated fanatic, or the culmination of a plot engineered by foreign powers.

# Le Grand Siècle

Louis XIII (1610–1643) succeeded his father after the king's tragic death in 1610. As he was nine years old at the time, Louis' regency was conferred by Parliament to the queen, Marie de' Medici, whose rule was influenced by a Florentine adventurer named Concino Concini. The queen purchased the Duke of Luxembourg's property and in 1615 commissioned the architect Salomon de Brosse to extend the structure into a palace. However, it was not completed until 1631, the date of her final exile, and Marie de' Medici never lived in this magnificent residence, which retained the Luxembourg name.

The Luxembourg Palace resembled a château: the entrance pavilion was covered by a dome and opened on to a *cour d'honneur* (court of honour), which led into the main building. The architect Salomon de Brosse combined this classically French layout with façades exhibiting a rustic *bossage* finish, which imitated the style of the Pitti Palace in Florence, of which Marie de' Medici had many happy memories. The palace interior was decorated with a series of paintings by the Flemish artist Peter Paul Rubens, depicting events marking her reign. The gardens were designed in a formal style by Jacques Boyceau, characterized by *parterres de broderies* (embroidered parterres) and water features, and were turned into a public park in 1799, although the Medici fountain from that time was preserved.

Louis XIII came of age when he turned 14, and in 1615 he married Anne of Austria, the Spanish Infanta, and escaped the clutches of his mother. In 1617, he exiled his mother to Blois on a temporary basis and executed Concini. Backed by Armand-Jean Duplessis, Cardinal de Richelieu (1585–1642), the king passed decrees that would have a huge impact on society; for instance, he took measures to ensure that the ban on duelling was reaffirmed, the aristocracy was able to engage in trade without detriment to its social status, and titles were conferred on commoners. Confrontations between Catholics and Protestants flared up again during his reign, involving bloody clashes, most notably in the temple at Charenton in 1621.

At several locations in the city, which had a population of 410,000 in about 1635, clever speculators initiated a number of successful projects: in 1608, Claude Charlot built the road that bears his name on land plots sold by the Grand Priory of the Knights Templar. In 1614, Christophe Marie began selling plots of land on the Île Saint-Louis. He built two stone bridges (Pont Marie and Pont de la Tournelle), ringed the island with brick quays, laid out roads on an orthogonal grid, sold plots of land and constructed houses. Magistrates and financiers established their operations on the quays, in the Hôtels Lambert, Hesselin, and Sainctot, which were built around 1630 by Louis Le Vau to benefit from this charming location. The estate of Marguerite de Valois, inherited by Louis XIII, was given over to financiers in 1623, creating a boom in grand townhouses along the rue de Lille and rue de Verneuil, and on the Quai Malaquais and Quai Voltaire, which had recently been opened.

**LEFT** The Luxembourg Palace, seen here in an etching by the studio of Jacques Chéreau from the eighteenth century, has been the home of the Senate since 1801. The entrance of the palace is on 15 rue de Vaugirard in the 6th arrondissement.

**OPPOSITE** A pannelled room that was originally in the Cabinet Colbert de Villacerf in rue de Turenne and which was reconstructed in the Musée Carnavalet. Painted c. 1650, the woodwork is embellished with grotesques and elegant and colourful decorative borders which are inspired by the Renaissance.

In 1624, the king had the mediaeval parts of the Louvre demolished in order to build the Pavillon de l'Horloge, designed by Jacques Lemercier. To please his mother, in 1628 he created a three-laned, elm-lined avenue on the banks of the Seine, known as the Cours la Reine. On the advice of his doctor, Jean Héroard, and the botanist Guy de La Brosse, the king founded the Jardin du Roi in 1626, with the aim of growing medicinal plants that would teach organic chemistry to doctors and apothecaries. In 1640, the Jardin du Roi opened its doors to the public, displaying 800 cultivated plants and a man-made hillock known as the Labyrinth, which was planted

with Mediterranean herbs, green oaks, pine trees, boxwood, a vine maple and an impressive cedar of Lebanon. Later called the Jardin des Plantes, the garden reached its high point under the curatorship of the famous scholar, the Comte de Buffon, from 1739 until 1788.

The advancement of educational institutions was assisted by the growth of printed publications. In 1631, Louis XIII granted Théophraste Renaudot the privilege of printing *La Gazette de France*, which became the official government newspaper. On 27 January 1635, he founded the Académie Française, with the mission of improving and maintaining the understanding of the French language and compiling the *Dictionnaire de*

*la langue française* (*Dictionary of the French Language*).

Cardinal de Richelieu, the Principal of the Sorbonne, replaced the college's dilapidated buildings in 1626 and commissioned the Sainte-Ursule Chapel, where he was finally laid to rest in a tomb sculpted by François Girardon. To cover the chapel, in 1635 Jacques Lemercier built the first dome, constructed entirely of stone, which was punctuated by high windows and covered in slate and which, by luck, was saved during the extension work undertaken in 1900.

So that he could live nearer to the king, in 1629 Richelieu asked Lemercier to build the Palais Cardinal with a garden and a theatre,

which was inaugurated in 1641. The young King Louis XIV took refuge there during the Fronde rebellion (1648–52), and as a result it became known as the Palais Royal. The construction of this lavish residence triggered the sale of plots of land in the Richelieu quarter, surrounding the Church of Notre-Dame-des-Victoires, the foundation stone of which was laid by Louis XIII in 1629. Other churches sprang up, in particular those of Saint Joseph-des-Carmes (1616), Saint-Gervais (1623), Notre-Dame-de-Bonne-Nouvelle (1624), Saint-Paul-Saint-Louis (1627) and the Oratoire (1630). The churches remain testament to the extraordinary construction work of the seventeenth century.

**LEFT** The Garden of the King for the Culture of Medicinal Plants, as depicted in this watercoloured engraving by Frédéric Scalberge from 1636. The Museum d'histoire naturelle ( at 57 rue Cuvier in the 5th arrondissement) was built around it.

**ABOVE** An engraving by Nicolas de Larmessan, dating from the seventeenth century called *Costume of the patissier, costume of the musician and costume of the chef*.

**OVERLEAF** The Île Saint-Louis and the Pont Marie, painted by Jean-Baptiste Raguenet in 1757. After the collapse of two arches caused by a catastrophic flood in 1658, the bridge was rebuilt without houses on the island side.

# An Open City

On 16 May 1643, the five-year-old Dauphin, Louis-Dieudonné (the God-given) was crowned king under the name Louis XIV (1643–1715). Due to his young age when he acceded the throne, his mother Anne of Austria acted as regent, with the help of Jules Cardinal Mazarin (1602–1661), Louis XIV's godfather.

Anne of Austria had the Abbey of Val-de-Grâce built by way of thanks to the Virgin Mary for having granted her wish – to give her a son after 23 years of marriage. Works on the abbey started in 1645, based on plans by François Mansart, and continued under the guidance of Jacques Lemercier and Pierre Le Muet until 1669. With a forecourt and a park extending over eight hectares (20 acres), its buildings are structured around an inner courtyard and a splendid church decorated with sculptures by Michel Anguier and Philippe Buyster, glorifying the motherhood of the Virgin Mary. The magnificent Baroque dome was painted by Pierre Mignard and spans the high altar (a copy of Bernini's *Baldachin*, the original of which is in St Peter's Basilica in the Vatican City of Rome), while the Nativity of Jesus is displayed underneath.

The king's childhood was characterized by a permanent state of insecurity, caused by civil strife; he faced the opposition of Parliament and the princes' rebellion. During this rebellion, known as the Fronde (1648–52), the royal family withdrew for a time to the Palais Royal and the Château de Saint-Germain-en-Laye. Not far from the Palais Royal, Cardinal Mazarin acquired the Hôtel Tubeuf, which François Mansart converted for him. Two stacked galleries decorated in an Italianate style provided a backdrop for the cardinal's magnificent collections of paintings and art objects.

In 1652, Anne of Austria and the young Louis XIV moved to the Louvre Palace, which was refurbished by Louis Le Vau. On the ground floor of the Petite Galerie, the queen's summer apartment consisted of a suite of six interconnecting rooms, finished with stucco and frescoes in the Roman style by Giovanni Romanelli and Michel Anguier. Charles Le Brun decorated the king's bedchamber and the Galerie d'Apollon between 1660 and 1664, and Claude Perrault built the monumental façade with a peristyle of double columns to close off the Cour Carrée from 1668 to 1678. However, the Louvre Palace was abandoned by the king and left in an incomplete state, but was soon occupied by the Académie Française, the Académie Royale de Peinture et de Sculpture (Royal Academy of Painting and Sculpture), and from 1699 the art salons.

After coming of age in 1651, when he was just 13 years old, Louis XIV was crowned king on 7 June 1654 at Reims. His marriage in 1660 to his cousin Maria Theresa (1638–83), daughter of Philippe IV of Spain and Elisabeth of France, formed an alliance that guaranteed the Treaty of the Pyrenees, which put an end to the war with Spain. After Cardinal Mazarin's death in 1661, Louis XIV assumed power at the age of 23 and then reigned personally, surrounding himself with exceptional men, including Colbert, Louvois, Vauban and Turenne. The birth of the Dauphin Louis in 1661 was celebrated with a great carrousel (equestrian games), attended by 1,300 courtiers in costume.

**ABOVE** Queen Anne (formerly of Austria) shows off Louis XIV (the Dauphin until 1643) in this anonymous painting from the seventeenth century.

**OPPOSITE** The newly cleaned colonade of the Louvre, painted by Pierre-Antoine Demachy, c. 1773. The eastern façade nowadays looks out onto rue l'amiral-de-Coligny (1st arrondissement).

The event gave its name to the Carrousel Esplanade, which played host to this lavish festival in 1662.

The king bestowed a royal charter on the glass-makers Compagnie de Saint-Gobain, established in the Faubourg Saint-Antoine, and on the Gobelins Tapestry Manufactory, which was extended by Jean-Baptiste Colbert. Under the direction of Charles Le Brun, 250 tapestry-makers and weavers produced carpets, hangings, seat and sofa covers, and even silk panels, destined for the royal residences.

Meanwhile, Sébastien Le Prestre de Vauban oversaw the construction of three hundred strongholds on the borders, ensuring the defence of the realm, which led to a 1670 royal order to dismantle the inner rings of fortifications. The Paris *enceintes* dating from the thirteenth, fifteenth, and seventeenth centuries were demolished between 1686 and 1732, apart from the Tuileries bastion and La Bastille. On the site where they had been, Louis XIV created a large thoroughfare, spanning 37 m (120 ft) wide and stretching 4.4 km (2.7 miles) from Place de la Bastille to Place de la Madeleine.

**RIGHT** An episode during the Fronde from 1648–52, depicted in a French School painting from the seventeenth century. The king's troops, commanded by Turenne, clashed with the Frondeurs commanded by the Prince de Condé in front of the Bastille.

This route, nicknamed the Grands Boulevards, was completed according to Pierre Bullet's plan between 1668 and 1705. Measuring 20 m (65 ft) wide, the paved road is reserved for traffic and flanked by two tree-lined sidewalks for pedestrians, embellished by the arches of Porte Saint-Denis and Porte Saint-Martin. Inspired by antiquity, these monumental gates take the shape of triumphal arches, symbolizing the passage between the city and the suburbs, and glorifying the deeds of royal armies. In 1672, François Blondel built the Porte Saint-Denis, on which Michel Anguier depicted the victories achieved in the Netherlands, and in 1674, Pierre Bullet erected the Porte Saint-Martin, with bas-reliefs celebrating the conquest of Franche-Comté.

On the site of the Tour de Nesle, the guard tower of the old city wall on the Left Bank *enceinte*, Le Vau built the Collège des Quatre-Nations (now the Institut de France), funded by Cardinal Mazarin before he died. Two concave wings, complete with two pavilions, frame the central chapel. Opened in 1688, the institution offered a university education to 60 gentlemen, complemented by lessons in weaponry, horseriding and dance. Mazarin's tomb, designed by Jules Hardouin-Mansart, rests in the chapel, whose cupola now stands as the symbol of the Académie Française.

**OPPOSITE** The Gallery of Apollo in the Louvre Museum. Decorated by Le Brun based on the theme of the course of the sun under the guidance of Apollo, this gallery was copied 20 years later at Versailles.

**BELOW** A tapestry depicting the visit of Louis XIV to the Gobelins Factory (42 avenue des Gobelins, 13th arrondissement) on 15 October 1667 from the workshop of Etienne Le Blond and forming part of the *Suite de l'Histoire du Roi*, 1729–34.

# The Glory of the Sun King

As the seventeenth century progressed and Paris's inner fortications were demolished under the reign of Louis XIV, the Sun King (Roi Soleil), as he became known, the city flourished and continued to expand westwards. The burgeoning growth took a new turn with the creation of the Champs-Elysées and its link to the Tuileries Gardens.

André Le Nôtre created this garden by planting an avenue of chestnut trees, 300 m (985 ft) long, along the medial axis of the Tuileries Palace, which was designed by Louis Le Vau and François d'Orbay between 1659 and 1672. This pathway directed the eye toward an octagonal basin and beyond to the Place Charles de Gaulle. The terrace at the end of the garden offered a magnificent panorama over the banks of the Seine and the Cours la-Reine, reaching the vast cultivated plain to the west.

In 1667, Le Nôtre transformed this agricultural land into landscaped gardens, thereby extending the view from the Tuileries Gardens to the Champs-Elysées roundabout with a straight avenue lined by a double row of elms. This great east–west axis was named the Avenue des Champs-Elysées in 1694. The thoroughfare extended as far as Pont de Neuilly by the eighteenth century, and strongly signalled the urbanization of Paris.

**BELOW** Colbert presents members of the Royal Academy of Sciences, created in 1667, to Louis XIV in this painting by Henri Testelin. The observatory in the background was built to stand apart from other buildings and chimneys at 61 rue de l'Observatoire in the 14th arrondissement.

**RIGHT** An engraving, signed by Gérard Jollain, of an Almanac for the Year of Grace MDCCVII (1707). The Royal Church of the Invalides dedicated by His Eminence Monseigneur the Cardinal de Noailles under invocation of Saint Louis on 22 August and visited by his Majesty on 28 August.

The Dauphin, the King and the Duke of Burgundy are featured in the first row under the dome of the church; on the left are the Cardinal de Noailles and the Duchess of Orléans; on the right, the architect Mansart is presenting the King with the key to the institution. In the lower part of the poster – created for the glory of the King – the calendar for the year is placed, showing the days of the week, Sundays, religious festivals and lunar cycles; it is framed by vignettes representing two aerial views of the Hôtel des Invalides, its refectory and soldiers exercising.

In 1666, Louis XIV founded the Académie Royale des Sciences and the following year he created the Paris Observatory to house astronomical instruments and further scientific research. On 21 June 1667, mathematicians drew on the ground the meridian that forms the axis of the main cubic field. Claude Perrault began the construction of the observatory in 1667 after converting 28-m (90-ft) deep quarries into temperate cellars suitable for experiments. From 1669 to 1683, the Italian astronomer Jean-Dominique Cassini made modifications to the building. The structure, built entirely in stone, attracted great admiration. The observatory was especially praised for its staircase, with suspended vaults, and its terrace with huge poles on to which the astronomers attached their telescopes.

However, such architectural expansion came in the wake of civil unrest. The Fronde rebellion unleashed great suffering, with around 40,000 destitute people forced to wander the streets during the 1650s. To re-establish public order, a ruling in 1656 prohibited begging and led to the foundation of the Hôpital Général (General Hospital), with the mission of interning poor folk on the fringes of society and vagrants – either willingly, or by force – and putting them to work, forcing them to earn their salvation. The law on locking up the poor, issued in 1657, led to the incarceration of 800 people in the disused premises of the Arsenal de la Salpêtrière on the outskirts of the city.

Antoine Duval, Louis Le Vau and Libéral Bruant were given the task of replacing this provisional detention centre with a gigantic institution. The architects designed the building between 1658 and 1678, drawing inspiration from the typology of a hospital in their grid layout. They grouped dormitories, dairies, sheds, stables and workshops around the austere chapel dedicated to St Louis. Notably, prostitutes were incarcerated in a prison, and then subjected to forced labour and severe punishments. Ten thousand people were confined to the Hôpital de la Salpêtrière in 1789, the year of the French Revolution.

In 1670, Louis XIV created the Hôtel des Invalides in order to accommodate 4,000 maimed war veterans, providing care and supervision to meet both military and religious needs. The main façade of the building is decorated with the image of Louis XIV in warrior dress and with *lucarnes* (small dormer windows), which are reminiscent of armoured busts. Bruant laid out dormitories, refectories, workshops and a hospital for 100 severely injured veterans around the 17 courtyards.

Between 1677 and 1706, Jules Hardouin-Mansart built the church of Saint-Louis-des-Invalides with its 107-m (350-ft) high dome, a masterpiece of Classical French architecture. It was regilded in 1989, at the time of the bicentenary of the French Revolution. Today, there are two separate churches: the "soldiers' church", with a sweeping, austere nave housing military figures in its galleries; and the dome church, which functions as the royal sanctuary. The dome church was distinguished by well-proportioned, restrained façades and lavish fittings, designed by Jean Jouvenet, Noël Coypel, François Girardon, Antoine Coysevox and Nicolas Coustou, although it was changed somewhat by the installation of Napoleon's tomb in 1840.

On 6 May 1682, the Sun King moved officially to Versailles with the court. After the death of Queen Maria Theresa in 1683, he secretly married Françoise d'Aubigné, the Marquise de Maintenon. In Paris, further embellishments glorifying the king were added under the supervision of Hardouin-Mansart, who designed two royal squares in a Classical style: the Place des Victoires (1686), which showcased a standing statue of Louis XIV by Martin Desjardins; and the Place Vendôme (1685–1720), where the equestrian statue of the Sun King took centre stage in 1699. Meanwhile, the construction of Pont Royal in 1689, following a design by Hardouin-Mansart, led the aristocracy to move into Faubourg Saint-Germain.

As the seventeenth century rolled on, Paris became an open, more extensive city, lit by around 2,700 candle lanterns, marked by boundaries set in 1672 and divided into 20 districts by a royal decree of 1702. The opening up of the city along two magnificent avenues, the Cours de Vincennes to the east and the Champs-Elysées to the west, improved access to previously unseen attractions – royal edifices, grand boulevards, streets lined with grand townhouses and world-famous monuments – thanks to the genius of its architects and the outstanding skills of its artists.

**ABOVE** A view of Paris from the Quai de la Rapée, painted by Pierre-Denis Martin in 1716. The hospice of la Salpêtrière, of which the dome can be seen, stands out on the Left Bank. Today, the establishment is part of the Groupe Hospitalier Pitié-Salpêtrière, 91–105 Boulevard de l'Hôpital, 13th arrondissement.

**OPPOSITE** The transportation of the statue of Louis XIV created by François Girardon on the Place Louis-le-Grand on 16 July 1699, painted by René-Antoine Houasse. This bronze equestrian statue ornamented the Place Vendôme (1st arrondissement). It was pulled down in 1792 and replaced by the Vendôme Column, which was erected to the glory of Napoléon I.

# The Age of Enlightenment

When Louis XIV died in 1715, the heir to the throne, his great-grandson Louis XV (1710–74), was only five years old. So his uncle, Philippe, Duke of Orléans, acted as regent until 1723. He lived in the Palais Royal in Paris, and in 1716 consented to throwing a public masked ball three times a week in the Salle de l'Opéra in the palace. A financial scandal erupted in 1720 when it proved impossible for the national banking system to exchange paper money for gold for clients, and it emerged that the Controller General of Finances, John Law, was responsible for its failure. In the meantime, the young Louis XV lived in the Tuileries Palace until 15 June 1722, at which point the king and court returned to the Château of Versailles.

Paris extended westwards, along the Left Bank in Faubourg Saint-Germain, and on the Right Bank in the Faubourgs Saint-Honoré, Poissonnière and Chaussée d'Antin. The aristocracy favoured the district of Saint-Germain over the Marais, and built magnificent townhouses (*hôtels*) with courtyards to the front and gardens at the back. Around 50 of these *hôtels* are still standing, and have been turned into governmental institutions, such as the Ministries for Agriculture and Social Affairs, foreign embassies – including those of the Netherlands and Switzerland – and museums. The Hôtel Matignon at 57 rue de Varenne in the 7th arrondissement, built in 1722 by Jean Courtonne, is the official residence of the Prime Minister. The Hôtel Biron at 77 rue de Varenne, built in 1730 by Jean Aubert, now houses the Musée Rodin (a museum dedicated to Auguste Rodin, who brought life to the French Classical tradition of sculpture). Meanwhile, between 1726 and 1730, Louise-Françoise de Bourbon – the eldest daughter of Louis XIV and his famous mistress Madame de Montespan – and her lover the Marquis de Lassay commissioned the building of the Palais Bourbon and the adjacent Hôtel de Lassay so that they could live in close proximity. The architects Giardini, Lassurance, Jacques V. Gabriel and Jean Aubert designed the residences for the couple.

**ABOVE RIGHT** Louis XV (1710–74), King of France, painted after Louis-Michel van Loo (1707–71).

**RIGHT** An eighteenth-century coloured engraving by Daumont of the garden of the Hôtel d'Evreux, which was owned by the Marquise de Pompadour. The hôtel (55 rue du Faubourg Saint-Honoré, 8th arrondissement) with its garden that backed onto the Champs-Elysées was acquired by Madame de Pompadour and bequeathed by her to Louis XV. It is now the Palais de l'Elysée and has been the official residence of the President of the Republic since 1874.

**OPPOSITE** A portrait by François Boucher (1721–64) of the Marquise de Pompadour, who was born Jeanne Antoinette Poisson, from 1757.

**OPPOSITE ABOVE** The ceremony of the laying of the first stone of the new Church of Sainte-Geneviève on 6 September 1764 painted by Pierre-Antoine Demachy (1723–1807). Louis XV laid the first stone of what is actually the Panthéon. Soufflot and the Marquis de Marigny, the Director of the King's Buildings, can be seen showing the king the building plans in front of a large model created especially for the ceremony.

**OPPOSITE BELOW** L'Hôtel de la Monnaie (the Treasury), situated at 11 Quai de Conti (6th arrondissement), painted by Pierre-Antonie Demachy. This superb neoclassical building with a terraced roof is now the Musée de la Monnaie et de la Medaille.

**BELOW** Part of the decorations in the salon of the engraver Gilles Demarteau, dating from c. 1765. Demarteau, who died in 1776, asked François Boucher, who was aided by Jean-Baptiste Huet and Jean-Honoré Fragonard, to create these countryside scenes for his shop in 1765.

Later, the Marquise de Pompadour, who became the king's mistress in 1745, set up home in the Faubourg Saint-Honoré, another area favoured by the aristocracy. In 1753, she purchased the Hôtel d'Evreux (now the Elysée Palace), which was originally built for the financier Antoine Crozat by Claude-Armand Mollet in 1718–20. Her brother, the Marquis de Marigny, was appointed Director General of the King's Buildings (the equivalent of the Minister of Culture) in 1751.

Although Louis XV lived in the Château de Versailles, throughout his long reign he was keen to make improvements to the capital and ordered the construction of famous monuments. The city of Paris wanted to erect an equestrian statue of the king, a commission awarded to Edme Bouchardon in 1748. In 1750, the king provided the land for the square that would later be graced with this statue, the Place Louis XV (now Place de la Concorde). He asked the principal royal architect, Ange-Jacques Gabriel (1698–1782), to summarize the projects submitted by his colleagues for the design competition for the square, which was inaugurated on 20 June 1763.

Louis XV was responsible for the foundation of the military school, the École Militaire at Place de Fontenoy and Place Joffre in the 7th arrondissement, on 13 January 1751, as a means of rewarding the *noblesse d'épée* (old military aristocracy). He derived inspiration for this project from the financier Joseph Pâris-Duverney and was supported by the Marquise de Pompadour. Ange-Jacques Gabriel began work on the institution, which was completed by Étienne-Louis Boullée, and then Alexandre-Théodore Brongniart in 1780.

Following a serious illness in 1744, Louis XV vowed that he would build a new church to replace the Abbey of Sainte-Geneviève, which had become terribly run down. The Marquis de Marigny entrusted the architect Jacques-Germain Soufflot (1713–80) with the construction of the church (now the Panthéon), for which Louis XV himself laid the foundation stone in 1764, and the building was completed in 1790.

At this time, the veritable palace of the Hôtel de la Monnaie was built by Jacques-Denis Antoine at 11 Quai de Conti in the 6th arrondissement, between 1767 and 1775, to produce the coins and medals of the empire. The École de Chirurgie (School of Surgery) was established by Jacques Gondoin at 12 rue de l'Ecole de Médecine in the 6th arrondissement in the same era (1769–74), complete with a wonderful amphitheatre (now occupied by University of Paris V).

**ABOVE** The furniture-maker Charles François Normand created this armchair for Voltaire. From 5 February 1778, the philosopher lived at the house of his friends the Marquis and Marquise de Villette, which is situated at 27 Quai Voltaire in the 7th arrondissement. It was here that he died on 30 May 1778.

**RIGHT** A Reading of the tragedy *L'Orphelin de la Chine* by Voltaire in the Salon of Madame Geoffrin in 1755, painted by Anicet Charles Gabriel Lemonnier (1743–1824), 1812. Marie-Thérèse Geoffrin is sitting on the right of the first row. The actor Lekain reads the story by Voltaire who was still in exile and whose bust is seen in the middle of the salon. Fontenelle, Montesquieu, Diderot and Marmontel figured among the guests.

Also running along the Left Bank are the Boulevards du Midi, which were built as counterparts to the Grands Boulevards on the Right Bank in 1760. These include the Boulevard des Invalides, Boulevard du Montparnasse, the section of Boulevard Raspail between Boulevard du Montparnasse and Place Denfert-Rochereau, as well as Boulevards Saint-Jacques, Auguste-Blanqui and de l'Hôpital.

The spectacular array of architectural work was intrinsic to an era known as the Enlightenment. The philosophers Voltaire, Jean-Jacques Rousseau and Denis Diderot characterized the thinking of this period in their writings. From 1749 to 1772, Diderot and Jean le Rond d'Alembert took on the mammoth task of publishing *L'Encyclopédie ou Dictionnaire raisonné des sciences, des arts et des métiers* (Encyclopaedia, or classified dictionary of the sciences, arts and crafts), which included contributions from more than 140 authors and 5,565 entries written by Diderot himself.

This era saw the emergence of salons, held mainly by aristocratic and bourgeois women, such as Madame de Lambert and Madame de Tencin. They welcomed painters, philosophers, writers and musicians into their circles. Madame Geoffrin (1699–1777), who provided financial support for *L'Encyclopédie*, received d'Alembert, Marivaux, Boucher, Hubert Robert and Van Loo in her salon at 374 rue Saint-Honoré in the 1st arrondissement. The cultural relationships the salon fostered assisted the growth of the arts.

**ABOVE** The Paris Streets Carnival, painted by Etienne Jeaurat (1699–1789), 1757. Onlookers as well as the water carrier (front, left) watch the Mardi Gras procession as it moves to the beat of the tambour player.

**RIGHT** An anonymous engraving of the "true sounds of Paris… as they are found in the town and suburbs of Paris", published by Pierre Leloup (circa 1760). Merchants walked about the streets advertising the sale of their goods by shouting out the name of the products on offer, including fish (salmon, eel, whiting), fruit (pears, redcurrants, hazelnuts), water and vinegar.

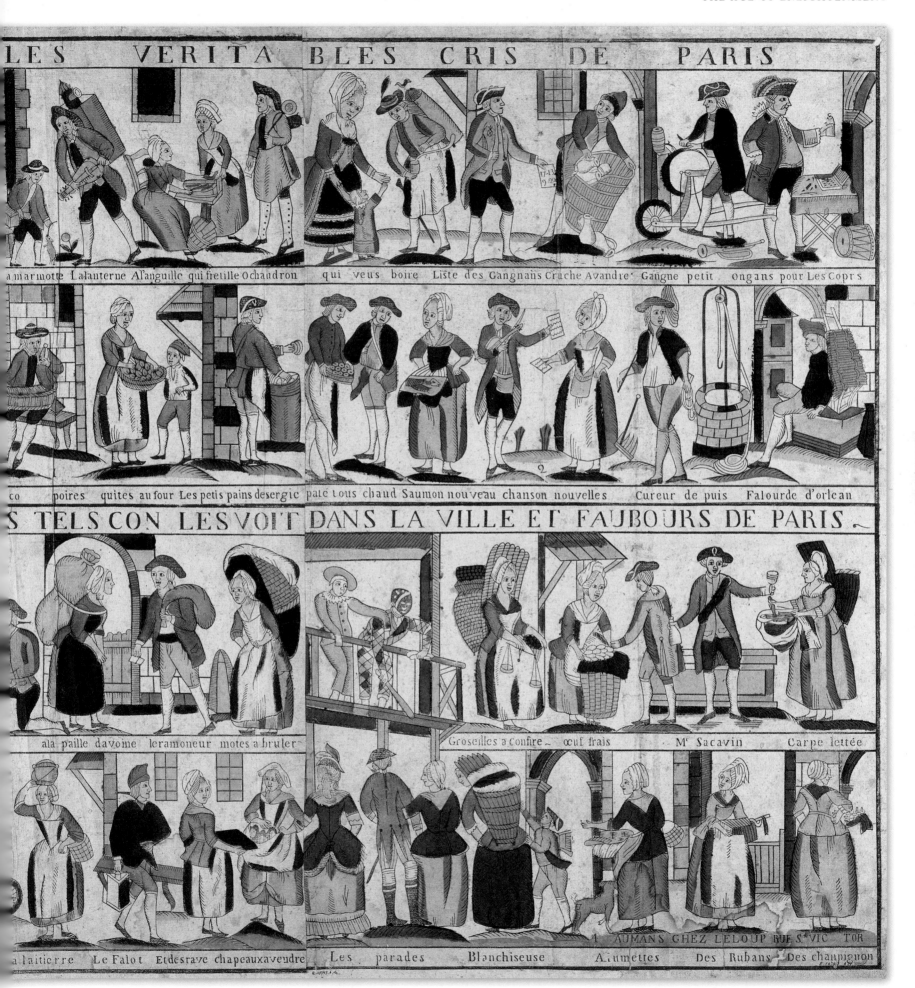

LES VERITA BLES CRIS DE PARIS

a marmotte Lalanterne Al'anguille qui fretille O chaudron     qui veu's boire  Liste des Gangnans Cruche Avandre  Gagne petit  ongans pour Les Coprs

co      poires   quites au four Les petis pains desergic  paté tous chaud Saumon nouveau chanson nouvelles   Cureur de puis   Falourde d'orlean

S TELS CON LES VOIT DANS LA VILLE ET FAUBOURS DE PARIS

a la paille davoine  leramoneur  motes a bruler        Groseilles a Confire   œuf frais       Mr Sacavin       Carpe lettée

a laitierre   Le Falot  Et desrave chapeaux avendre   Les   parades    Blanchiseuse     Alumettes    Des Rubans  Des champiguon

# The Reign of Louis XVI

Louis XVI (1754–93), the grandson of Louis XV, succeeded to the throne of France in 1774 at the age of twenty. Four years earlier he had married the Archduchess Marie-Antoinette of Austria (1755–93), who was then 15 years old and the daughter of Emperor Francis I and his wife Maria Theresa. Louis XVI and Marie-Antoinette lived in the Château of Versailles until 1789.

Town planning projects in the capital continued unabated, notably in the Faubourg Saint-Germain, where a bridge was built by Jean-Rodolphe Perronet from 1789 to 1791 to link it to the right bank, known as the Pont Louis XVI (now Pont de la Concorde). In 1782, Prince Frédéric III of Salm-Kyrbourg commissioned the architect Pierre Rousseau to build the Hôtel de Salm (now the Musée de la Légion d'Honneur at 2 rue de la Légion d'Honneur in the 7th arrondissement).

The architects Marie-Joseph Peyre and Charles de Wailly completed the Théâtre Français (now Théâtre de l'Odéon at the Place de l'Odéon in the 6th arrondissement), which became the new home of the Comédiens Français company, which was inaugurated on 9 April 1782 with Racine's tragedy, *Iphigénie*. It was in this theatre that the controversial play *La Folle journée ou Le Mariage de Figaro* (1778) by Pierre Augustin Caron de Beaumarchais (1732–1799) was performed on 27 April 1784, following a two-year ban by Louis XVI, due to objections about the subversive nature of the work. The premiere was a great success, and a crush of 4,000–5,000 people tried to get in to what was one of the most significant events in the history of French theatre.

Business ventures sprang up in the form of cafés, thanks to the craze for the delicious beverage of the same name, *du café*

**BELOW** The demolition of the houses on the Pont Notre-Dame in 1786 is depicted in this painting by Hubert Robert (1733–1808). For security and hygiene reasons, it was decided to stop the building of houses on bridges in 1786.

**RIGHT** A detail from a view of the Café Caveau at the Palais Royal made in the eighteenth century. The café, which was decorated with large mirrors and the busts of Clück, Guétry and Piccini, brought opera lovers together.

**BELOW** A poster advertising the 76th performance of Beaumarchais' *The Marriage of Figaro* on 21 August 1785 by the Comédie-Française. The play by Pierre-Augustin Caron de Beaumarchais was so successful after the premiere on 27 April 1784 at the Comédie-Française (then located in Place de l'Odéon) that it was performed again in the years that followed.

LES COMEDIENS
ORDINAIRES DU ROI
DONNERONT aujourd'hui Dimanche 21 Août 1785,
LE ROI LEAR, Tragédie de M. Ducis,
Suivie DE LA COMTESSE D'ESCARBAGNAS,
Comédie en un Acte, de MOLIÈRE, avec un Divertissement.
Demain, la soixante-seizieme Représentation
DE LA FOLLE JOURNÉE,
OU LE MARIAGE DE FIGARO
Comédie nouvelle en cinq Actes, avec un Divertissement.
Mercredi 24, la septieme Représentation du JALOUX SANS AMOUR,
Comédie en cinq Actes, en vers;
Et la quatrieme DE MELCOUR ET VERSEUIL,
Comédie nouvelle en un Acte, en vers.

(coffee). This drink became fashionable in 1669, when the Turkish ambassador Soliman Aga, who had come to visit the court of Louis XIV, brought coffee with him and gave it to his guests to taste. In 1672, Pascal Harouthioun offered coffee-tasting sessions in his shop in the fair of Saint-Germain, but it was Café Procope, founded in 1686 by Italian-born Francesco Procopio dei Coltelli (who used his French name Procope) at 13 rue de l'Ancienne Comédie in the 6th arrondissement, which gave a real boost to these establishments. Voltaire, Jean-Jacques Rousseau, Diderot, Danton, Robespierre, Marat and Benjamin Franklin all frequented the lavishly decorated café. At the Palais Royal, the Foy and Du Caveau cafés grew up alongside restaurants such as Beauvilliers and Véfour, in the galleries built in 1784 by Victor Louis.

Aeronautical events proved popular with residents of Paris: paper manufacturers, brothers Joseph and Étienne Montgolfier, invented the first airships called *montgolfières* (balloons filled with hot air) and the physicist Jacques Alexandre Charles perfected the Montgolfiers' invention by replacing the hot air with hydrogen. Balloons were launched in 1783 from the garden of the wallpaper manufacturer Jean-Baptiste Réveillon at 31 rue de Montreuil in the 11th arrondissement. On 21 November that year, the first manned free flight carrying Jean-François Pilâtre de Rozier and the Marquis d'Arlandes left Château de La Muette in the 16th arrondissement for the Butte aux Cailles in the 13th arrondissement, taking 25 minutes to cross a distance of 12 km (7 miles).

Another *enceinte* – the *enceinte des Fermiers Généraux* (the Wall of the Farmers-General) was built in 1784. However, this *enceinte* was fiscal rather than defensive, comprising around 50 customs offices, which acted as barriers where tolls were levied on goods coming into the city. Claude-Nicolas Ledoux, the architect of the Royal Saltworks at Arc-et-Senans (in the Doubs département), designed these barriers for purposes of trade. However, only four barriers remain due to the destruction in 1860: the Barrière d'Enfer (1 Avenue du Colonel Rol-Tanguy, 14th arrondissement), the rotunda of la Villette (Place de Stalingrad, 19th arrondissement), the rotunda of Orléans or Parc Monceau (Place de la République-Dominicaine, 8th arrondissement) and the Barrière du Trône (Place de la Nation, 11th and 12th arrondissements).

As the eighteenth century progressed, the French regime was weakened by social and economic instability. Public debt worsened and the aristocracy refused to introduce the necessary reforms to improve the lot of the city's population. Consequently, Louis XVI and Marie-Antoinette, in particular, became increasingly unpopular, and tensions in Paris escalated due to problems in obtaining essential supplies and the high price of bread.

**LEFT** Joseph-Silfrède Duplessis's (1725–1802) portrait of Louix XVI in his coronation robes. Louis XVI was crowned in Reims on 11 June 1775.

**OPPOSITE** Queen Marie-Antoinette in a blue dress and white skirt sits holding a book. This is a detail of the 1788 portrait by Elisabeth Vigée-Le Brun (1755–1842).

## SIGNS

In olden days, signs were hung on the façade of almost every house or shop. They indicated where someone lived, and assisted residents and visitors in finding their way around Paris before a precise system of street numbering was introduced in accordance with a decree of 1805. Signs frequently indicated the product made or sold by craftsman: a key represented a locksmith and a wheatsheaf signified a baker's shop. They also depicted themes from history, religion, the animal kingdom (horses, lions and cockerels), or the plant world (grapes and pine cones). Many roads still bear the name of a sign to this day, such as rue du Chat-qui-Pêche (Street of the Fishing Cat) and rue du Plat-d'Etain (Street of the Pewter Dish).

**OPPOSITE** The balloon ascension of Charles and Robert in the Tuileries on 1 December 1783. The physician Jacques Alexandre Charles and the medical instrument maker Robert the Younger took off in a hydrogen-filled balloon from the Tuileries Gardens. After a flight of two hours and 45 minutes they landed at Nesles-la-Vallée, some 30 km (18½ miles) from Paris.

**ABOVE** The Orléans or Parc Monceau Rotonda in the Place de la République-Dominicaine in the 8th arrondissement. Situated at the entrance to Parc Monceau, it is one of the four customs controls that were built by Ledoux (1736–1806) and which have been conserved in the capital. Begun in 1787, the rotunda was altered in 1860 by the addition of a dome and ribbed columns.

**RIGHT** An eighteenth-century wine merchant's sign made out of wrought iron. It says "*A la petite hote [hotte]*" ("To the little basket").

# The French Revolution

The Réveillon riot erupted during 26–28 April 1789, in the run up to the French Revolution. Réveillon was a wallpaper manufacturer who proposed lifting the tax on goods, resulting in a fall in salaries. Workers and unemployed residents in the Faubourg Saint-Antoine rose up in protest at this proposal at a time when the cost of bread, their staple diet, had risen to an exorbitant level. This bread riot left 100 dead and almost 300 injured. Réveillon, whose house was burned down, sought refuge in the Bastille. He was the only person that year to enter it willingly.

On 12 July 1789, Louis XVI unleashed a wave of demonstrations against the government when he dismissed Jacques Necker, the Director General of Finances and an advocate of reform. During the night many of the city's tollhouses were set on fire. The next day, the electorate set up a bourgeois militia, numbering 48,000 men, to protect the capital and ensure its security. In order to arm this militia, Parisians seized the 32,000 rifles and 12 cannon stockpiled in the Hôtel des Invalides on 14 July. They proceeded to the Bastille, where the ammunition and gunpowder needed for these weapons were kept.

When the prison governor, De Launay, refused to let them in, they attacked the fortress. This storming of the Bastille left 73 people injured and around 100 dead, including the governor, who was killed by the crowd. Yet only seven prisoners were being held in the Bastille: four forgers, two madmen and an aristocrat, imprisoned at the request of this family. The forgers soon slipped away, whereas the lunatics and the aristocrat were borne aloft by the triumphant crowd: the two madmen returned to the Charenton asylum the following day, and the aristocrat spent the rest of his days in the provinces.

On 15 July, the entrepreneur Pierre-François Palloy (1755–1835) took the initiative and began the demolition of the Bastille, with the help of a team of 700 workmen. The astronomer Jean-Sylvain Bailly (1736–93) was elected Mayor of Paris and the bourgeois militia took over as the National Guard under the

**BELOW LEFT** An engraving by Georges Pélicier and Claude Niquet of the *Gunfire on the Faubourg Saint-Antoine, 28 April 1789 – The Reveillon Affair.* Guards fired on the rioters who threw stones from their houses above. In the centre, the small building is the fountain at 1 rue de Montreuil in the 11th arrondissement. In the background on the right is one of the two columns of the Trône customs control (now in Place de la Nation), the work of Ledoux which was still not finished.

command of General de La Fayette. On 16 July, the king recalled Jacques Necker as the finance minister, who resigned on 4 September 1790. As their rhetoric, the National Assembly adopted *The Declaration of the Rights of Man and of the Citizen* on 26 August 1789. The treatise has 17 articles, the first of which states that all men are born free and have equal rights. It would have a massive impact on the rest of the world.

On 5 October, around 6,000 female citizens marched to Versailles in the company of La Fayette at the head of the National Guard, in order to demand bread from the king, queen and dauphin, who were commonly nicknamed the Baker, his Wife and their little Apprentice. The following day, on 6 October 1789, the king and royal family were forced by the crowd to leave the Château of Versailles and moved to the Tuileries Palace for a while. At nearly midnight on 20 June 1791, Louis XVI and his family secretly left the Tuileries in a covered carriage heading for

**BELOW** The Storming of the Bastille, 14 July 1789, painted by Jean-Baptiste Lallemand (1716–1803).

# THE BASTILLE

On Cardinal de Richelieu's initiative, the fortress built in 1370 was converted during the seventeenth century into a state prison for individuals who were a threat to the kingdom's security. They were incarcerated in the Bastille on the production of a *lettre de cachet* (sealed letter): they did not know the reason for their detention and were put there in secret. The Bastille became the symbol of the absolute monarchy's despotic rule. The finance minister Nicolas Fouquet, the Man in the Iron Mask, Voltaire and the Marquis de Sade were all imprisoned there. After the demolition of Charles V's *enceinte* in 1670, the Bastille had lost any defensive function. There were plans to knock it down in 1784 as it only held a few prisoners and its running costs were prohibitive.

**ABOVE** The Festival of the Federation, 14 July 1790 by Charles Thévenin (1764–1838), 1796. The Festival of the Federation, in the Champ de Mars, celebrated the first anniversary of the taking of the Bastille. Louis XVI took the oath to the constitution, with Bailly, the Mayor of Paris, by his side and La Fayette standing in front at the head of the troops. Marie-Antoinette is shown on the right with the dauphin in her arms.

**LEFT** An exercise book belonging to the Dauphin (Louis XVII), 1785–95, which dates from circa 1790–92. The Dauphin, the son of Louis XVI and Marie-Antoinette, learned to read at the age of four. He did his writing exercises under the supervision of M. Dessales (or de Salle). He corrected this notebook made up of ten sheets in the Tuileries Palace. The Dauphin died aged 10 in the Temple Tower.

**BELOW** One of Marie-Antoinette's shoes. It was snatched from the hands of one of the invaders of the Tuileries on 10 August 1792 by M. d'Ennery de Champuis, who defended the Tuileries as a grenadier.

Montmédy near the Luxembourg border, to rendezvous with troops loyal to the king. But they were arrested on the evening of 21 June at Varennes (in the Meuse département) and brought back to Paris on 25 June. This flight only increased the population's mistrust of the king.

On 3 September 1791, the National Assembly passed the constitution to which the king swore the oath on 14 September 1791. Convinced of an alliance between the king and the Austrian and Prussian armies, the National Guards of Marseille and Brest joined the workers of Faubourg Saint-Antoine in seizing the Tuileries Palace on 10 August 1792. The capture of the Tuileries Palace signalled the fall of the monarchy.

The king and his family took refuge in the riding hall of the Legislative Assembly, known as the Salle du Manège, in the Tuileries Palace (situated along the Terrasse des Feuillants in front of 230 rue de Rivoli in the 1st arrondissement), where they stayed for four days. On the evening of 13 August 1792, Louis XVI, Marie-Antoinette, their two children (Madame Royale and the dauphin) and Princess Élisabeth, the king's sister, were taken to the Temple fortress and imprisoned in its tower.

**RIGHT** Buttons made from pieces of stone taken from the Bastille and painted. The entrepreneur Palloy created a series of products derived from the fortress's materials: keys, models of the Bastille, buttons etc. These buttons, representing the body of the City of Paris, are encased in laurel wood.

**BELOW** A drawing by Baron François Gérard (1770–1837) of the events of 10 August 1792. In the Assembly the crowd are pointing their fingers at Louis XVI and Marie-Antoinette (to the right of the drawing). The royal family sits in the Press Box of *Le Logographe* (which had been ordered to report on the debates), separated from the room by a grille and behind the armchair of Pierre Vergniaud who is presiding over the sitting.

# The Foundation of the Republic

The National Convention, as the fresh Assembly was called, abolished the monarchy and declared France a Republic on 22 September 1792. Louis XVI and Marie-Antoinette were put on trial and sentenced to death: Louis XVI was guillotined in Place de la Concorde on 21 January 1793 and Marie-Antoinette on 16 October 1793. Their son, the dauphin (who became Louis XVII on the death of his father) died at the age of ten in the Temple Fortress on 8 June 1795. The daughter of Louis XVI and Marie-Antoinette, Madame Royale (1778–1851), was the only surviving family member. She was exchanged in 1795 for Convention commissioners, who were being held abroad as prisoners of war, and married her cousin, the Duke of Angoulême, who was the eldest son of Charles X.

There were two opposing factions within the Convention – the Girondins and the Montagnards. The Girondins were moderate representatives, elected from the regions, including Jacques-Pierre Brissot and Pierre Vergniaud. The Montagnards (Mountain Men) were given this name because they sat on the highest benches. The group was made up of action-driven representatives elected from Paris, including Georges Danton, Jean-Paul Marat and Maximilien de Robespierre.

On 2 June 1793, the Girondin deputies were expelled from the Convention and most were subsequently arrested and executed. Just over a month later, on 13 July, Charlotte Corday (1768–93), a young aristocrat from Normandy, stabbed Marat, because she held him responsible for the persecution of the Girondins and the bloodshed during the Revolution. Corday was guillotined four days later, whereas Marat was seen as a martyr of the Revolution.

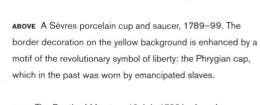

**ABOVE** A Sèvres porcelain cup and saucer, 1789–99. The border decoration on the yellow background is enhanced by a motif of the revolutionary symbol of liberty: the Phrygian cap, which in the past was worn by emancipated slaves.

**LEFT** *The Death of Marat on 13 July 1793* by Jean-Jacques Hauer (1751–1829), 1794. Charlotte Corday assassinated Jean-Paul Marat, the Montagnard deputy and editor of *L'Ami du peuple*, as he was taking a bath to ease a skin condition.

**OPPOSITE ABOVE** The planting of a Liberty Tree, a gouache by Etienne Béricourt, c. 1789. The planting of such a tree was a reason to celebrate. The tree would have been an oak or a poplar (whose Latin name meant "people").

In September 1793, Robespierre unleashed what became known as the Reign of Terror, as a means of combating the threats facing the Republic: foreign wars outside its borders and counter-revolution within the country. Many suspects were imprisoned and then guillotined. On the economic front, the "maximum law" of 29 September 1793 fixed the prices of staple foods and wages.

In 1794, the Montagnards tore each other apart. Robespierre and his followers eliminated their former allies, Georges Danton, Camille Desmoulins and Jacques René Hébert, who were all sent to the guillotine. On the night of 27–28 July 1794 (9–10 Thermidor Year 2), it was Robespierre's turn to be arrested and executed, along with the revolutionaries Louis de Saint-Just and Georges Couthon. After the fall of Robespierre, a new regime called the Directory was established between 1795 and 1799. Executive power was entrusted to a directorate of five members, each of whom had to be at least 40 years old.

In the wake of the Revolution, the architecture of the city changed. Paris's boundaries shifted towards a fresh alignment with the Wall of the Farmers-General on 21 May 1790, and the capital was divided up on 11 October 1795 into 48 sectors, grouped into 12 councils. Even though many works of art and religious buildings were destroyed during the Revolution, a fervent cultural life began to emerge, characterized by the foundation of new museums and the National Archives in 1790.

Symbols of the monarchy, the royal statues which adorned the squares of Paris, were all destroyed with one exception: a sculpture of Louis XIV dressed as a Roman emperor by Antoine Coysevox, inaugurated on 14 July 1689 (which now stands in the courtyard of Musée Carnavalet). It was decreed that the possessions of the clergy and émigrés belonged to the nation, so they were confiscated, sold or incorporated into state collections. Some buildings were demolished at that time, whereas others were reassigned: former convents were turned into schools, hospitals or prisons. The church of Sainte-Geneviève became the Pantheon on 4 April 1791, and was dedicated to the great men who served their country.

The painter Alexandre Lenoir saved works of art and remnants of churches from being destroyed, preserving them in a warehouse that was set up in the convent of the Grands Augustins (now the Ecole des Beaux-Arts at 14 rue Bonaparte in the 6th arrondissement). He was appointed director of this repository in 1791, which dealt exclusively with sculpture from 1793 and became the Musée des Monuments Français on 21 October 1795.

The day after the Tuileries Palace was stormed on 11 August 1792, a decree was passed, leading to the establishment of a museum in the Louvre Palace. The collections comprised artworks derived from the former Crown collections and the possessions seized from the clergy and émigrés. The Musée du Louvre was symbolically opened on 10 August 1793, the anniversary of the fall of the monarchy, although its actual public opening took place on 18 November 1793. The Jardin du Roi was reorganized on 10 June 1793 as the Museum d'Histoire Naturelle (Natural History Museum) to include provision for state education.

In the autumn of 1794, Abbot Henri Grégoire proposed the founding of a new institution to the National Convention: the Conservatoire des Arts et Métiers (National Conservatory of Arts and Crafts), bringing together machines, models, tools, drawings and books on the applied arts, manufacturing and commerce. The Conservatory was set up in 1798 in the former priory of Saint-Martin-des-Champs (at 292 rue Saint-Martin, 3rd arrondissement).

In 1794, the National Archives merged with the archives of the Ancien Régime, to preserve the history of the new government.

On 6 March 1808, Napoléon Bonaparte set up the Archives in the Hôtel de Soubise at 60 rue des Francs-Bourgeois in the 3rd arrondissement.

**ABOVE** *The Arrest of Robespierre on the Night of 9–10 Thermidor, Year II*, an engraving by Octave Tassaert (1765–1835) and Fulcran-Jean Harriet (died 1835), 1794. On 9 Thermidor, Year II (27 July 1794), Maximilien Robespierre, Antoine-Louis de Saint-Just and Georges Couthon were arrested by the Convention. Freed by their supporters, they took refuge in the Hôtel de Ville where troops loyal to the Convention attacked at night. Robespierre, wounded by two gunshots, was beheaded on 28 July 1794 in the Place de la Concorde.

**LEFT** The Grand Gallery of the Louvre during its restoration, painted by Hubert Robert (1733–1808). This painting shows the gallery as it was between April 1796 and April 1799. On the podium on the right is the statue of Zenon, which was taken during the Italian Campaign from the Capitoline Museum in Rome.

**OPPOSITE** A view of one of the rooms of the Musée des Monuments français (now the School of Fine Arts, 14 rue Bonaparte, 6th arrondissement), painted by the studio of Léon Matthieu Cochereau (1793–1817). On the left, stands the statue of Henri IV by Barthélemy Tremblay and on the right is the equestrian statue of Louis XIV by François Girardon.

# The Era of Napoléon I

**B**orn on 15 August 1769 in Ajaccio (Corsica), Napol´on Bonaparte took up a career in the military. In 1796, he married Joséphine de Beauharnais (1763–1814) and he was showered in glory during the Italian campaign. At the very moment at which the Directory was under threat of a royalist comeback, his military genius earned a degree of political clout that brought him to power in the coup d'état of 18 Brumaire (9–10 November 1799). During the Consulate (1800–04), headed by Napoléon, his associates Emmanuel-Joseph Sieyès and Roger Ducos tried their best to restore peace in the land by granting a general amnesty to émigrés and the freedom of worship to the clergy.

Several steps were taken to improve the welfare of Paris's population, which had reached 555,000 in 1801. The following year Bonaparte gave the order to dig out the Canal de l'Ourcq, thereby enabling water to pass through the Villette basin and supply the city's needs.

By 1808, this route fed 56 public fountains and 15 new water points, notably the Palmier Fountain. The cemeteries of Montparnasse and Père Lachaise were opened in 1801, and the Montmartre cemetery was extended.

Conscious of the steel industry's need for improvement, Bonaparte demanded that Pont des Arts, Pont de la Cité and Pont d'Austerlitz be constructed in cast iron. The Passerelle des Arts footbridge consisted of nine metal arches supporting a wooden superstructure that was lit and decorated with flowers, creating a "suspended garden". Restored to its original form in recent years, it is all that remains of this innovative structure, modelled on an English prototype.

**BELOW** The Fountain on the Place du Câtelet by Etienne Bouhot, 1810. The destruction of the Grand Châtelet freed space at the end of the Pont-au-Change (1st arroindissement), François-Jean Bralle built the Palmier Fountain there, which was topped by a statue of Victory executed by Simon-Louis Boizot.

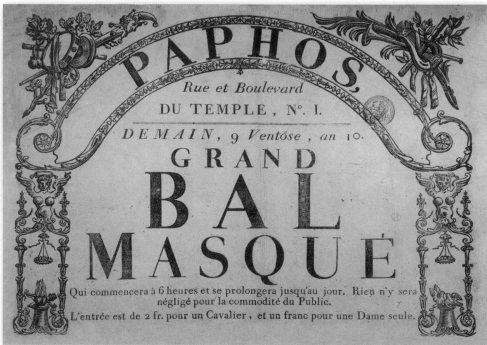

Appointed Consul for Life on 5 August 1802, Bonaparte lived in the royal apartments in the south wing of the Tuileries Palace. Charles Percier and Léonard Fontaine renovated the interior decoration and started work on the wing overlooking ´rue de Rivoli. This broad avenue was lined with beautiful, arcade-fronted stone buildings and linked in 1802–03 to Rue Saint-Honoré via rues de Castiglione, Cambon, de Mondivi and du Mont-Thabor. The rue de la Paix was laid out in 1806, completing a scheme that would turn residential land plots into a luxury retail sector. The properties' interior design set the trend for an Empire style, combining the repertoire of Classical and Egyptian forms with traditional decorative features.

On 18 May 1804, Napoléon Bonaparte was proclaimed Emperor of the French under the title Napoléon I and later sanctified in Notre-Dame Cathedral on 2 December in the presence of Pope Pius VII. He introduced the Civil Code and the Legion of Honour, founded secondary schools and organized the financial system by establishing the Banque de France, the revenue court and the stock exchange, La Bourse. Furthermore, he improved the distribution of goods by opening four covered markets, including the Saint-Germain market and the flower market on Quai de la Corse. Later, he restored the Académie Français, as part of the Institut de France, which occupied the Collège des Quatre-Nations. Its chapel included a statue of the Emperor by the sculptor Philippe-Laurent Roland.

Following in the footsteps of the Roman Emperors, Napoléon celebrated his resounding victory at Austerlitz on 2 December 1805 by building permanent monuments in the city. He erected a massive triumphal arch, known as the Arc de Triomphe, at the end of the Avenue des Champs-Elysées, laying its foundation stone on 15 August 1806. Jean-François Chalgrin designed the architectural plan of the monument in 1809. For Place du Carrousel, which lies on the central axis of the Tuileries Palace that burned down in 1871 and was razed in 1883, Napoléon commissioned a triumphal arch from Percier and Fontaine as a tribute to the Great Army. The resulting Arc de Triomphe du Carrousel was built from 1806 to 1809 in coloured stone and modelled on the ancient Arch of Septimius Severus in Rome; its sculpted bas-reliefs recall the glorious campaign of 1805.

**ABOVE LEFT** A plate from the Emperor's dinner service. It shows the rue de Rivoli which was built between the Place de la Concorde and the Place des Pyramides (1st arrondissement), and then continued for nearly 3 km (2 miles) to the rue Saint-Antoine (4th arrondissement).

**ABOVE** A poster advertising Paphos, a grand masked ball, in Year 10 of the Republic (1802). In 1795 the architect Bricard created an entertainment area at the junction of Boulevard du Temple and Rue du Temple, (now Place de la République). It took the form of a circular temple supported by Doric order columns. The garden, dance hall, café and gallery housed the audience who were charmed by "the Lilliputian mountains", fireworks, masked balls and roulette games.

**BELOW** A nineteenth-century watercolour by François-Etienne Villeret of the Seine, the Institute and the Pont des Arts. The Passerelle (footbridge) des Arts linked the Louvre Museum to the Institute and was rebuilt in 1984 using the same design but with seven archways to increase navigation.

In the centre of Place Vendôme, Jacques Gondouin and Jean-Baptiste Lepère erected a 43.5 m (143 ft) column between 1806 and 1810, based upon Trajan's Column in Rome. This stone column, topped by an effigy of Napoléon, is covered in bronze plaques taken from the cannons of the Russian and Austrian armies. The bas-reliefs carved on the plaques represent 76 episodes from military campaigns.

Meanwhile, Napoléon divorced Josephine in 1809, so that he could marry Marie-Louise de Habsbourg-Lorraine (1791–1847) on 2 April 1810. Marie-Louise gave him an heir, whom they called the "King of Rome" (1811–1832). The Emperor was at the forefront of reforms to street numbering and trade, and at the same time devised various monuments, which symbolized his reign. Alexandre-Théodore Brongniart designed one particular building – the Stock Exchange – inspired by the Classical basilica and the layout of markets. On 10 May 1811, the city was divided into 12 arrondissements (boroughs) and 48 quartiers (districts), an apportionment that remained in force until 1860.

However, defeat at the Battle of Waterloo on 18 June 1815 brought the fall of the Empire and Napoleon's exile to the island of St Helena, where he died on 5 May 1821. In his final will, he had written: "My wish is for my ashes to rest on the banks of the Seine, among the French people I have loved so dearly."

**RIGHT** A miniature portrait of Marie-Louise on leather by Salomon-Guillaume Counis, after Jean-Baptiste Isabey.

**OPPOSITE ABOVE** A review day during the Empire in 1810, painted by Joseph-Louis Bellangé and Adrien Dauzats in 1862. The statue on the top of the Arc du Carousel was taken in Constantinople in 1204 and transported to Venice where Napoléon seized it during his tour. Today, the Arc du Carrousel forms the entrance to the Tuileries Gardens.

**BELOW** *The Toppling of the Statue of Napoléon from the Triumphal Column in the Place Vendôme, 8 April 1814*, engraved by Georges-Emmanuel Optiz. This event followed the Senate's decision on 2 April which declared that Napoléon and his family had been deposed from the throne.

# The Restoration of the Monarchy

**O**n 1 April 1814, the provisional government announced the fall of Napoléon and restored the Bourbons to the throne. After an exile of 23 years, Louis XVIII (1755–1824), Louis XVI's brother, returned to Paris on 3 May 1814, making it the seat of the monarchy. He chose the Tuileries Palace as the royal residence, abandoning the Château of Versailles. However, his reign was violently interrupted on 19 March 1815 in a period known as the Hundred Days, during which Napoléon attempted to take power again, before finally abdicating on 22 June 1815. At Louis XVIII's death on 16 September 1824, his younger brother Charles X (1757–1836) succeeded him.

On 19 January 1816, Louis XVIII ordered the reinstatement of the royal statues, which had been pulled down during the French Revolution: in 1818 François-Frédéric Lemot cast a new statue of Henri IV for Place Dauphine; François-Joseph Bosio made one of Louis XIV for Place des Victoires in 1822; and in 1829 Louis Dupaty, then Jean-Pierre Cortot, completed the statue of Louis XIII for Place des Vosges.

In 1816, Louis XVIII entrusted Pierre-François-Léonard Fontaine with the construction of the expiatory chapel on the site of the Madeleine cemetery, where Louis XVI and Marie-Antoinette were buried. The Chapelle Expiatoire at 29 rue Pasquier in the 8th arrondissement was consecrated on 21 January 1824.

The Restoration witnessed the flourishing of *passages couverts* (arcades). These well-lit commercial galleries had the advantage of concentrating shops in one location and protected the window

shopper from inclement weather and traffic with a sheltered walkway. The first one to be built in Paris in 1786 was the Galerie de Bois next to the Palais Royal. However, its condition deteriorated rapidly, so it was replaced in 1828 with the Galerie d'Orléans, designed by the architect Fontaine. Galerie Colbert was built nearby in 1823, followed by the Vivienne and Véro-Dodat galleries in 1826. The Verdeau, des Panoramas and des Princes passages were located on the Grands Boulevards.

Three canals provided a navigation route on the Seine. The Canal de l'Ourcq and Canal Saint-Denis were started in 1805 and completed in 1821. Canal Saint-Martin was built under the direction of Charles-Edouard Devilliers and the engineers Tarbé and Brémontier, and inaugurated on 4 November 1825 by the king, Charles X. As a result, industrial zones developed alongside the canals, where heavy goods were unloaded.

As districts developed in Paris, they were given fashionable names, drawn from recent cultural history. Quartier François I, near the Champs-Elysées, and the Quartier de l'Europe, developed in 1824 for the bourgeoisie, adopted street names evoking large capital cities such as London, Amsterdam, Vienna, and Saint Petersburg. The residential district of Nouvelle Athènes (New Athens), which was delimited by rue des Martyrs, rue de La Rochefoucauld and rue Saint-Lazare in the 9th arrondissement, was given its name in 1823 by the poet Adolphe Dureau de la Malle. The artistic élite gathered there in houses designed in a style inspired by Antiquity. The Comédie-Française actors, in particular, Mademoiselle Mars, Mademoiselle Duchesnois and François Joseph Talma, lived in rue de la Tour-des-Dames, as did the painters Horace Vernet and Paul Delaroche. The writers Alexandre Dumas and George Sand, the composer Frédéric Chopin and the singer Pauline Garcia-Vardiot all lived in houses in Square d'Orléans in the 9th arrondissement, a private estate built in 1830 by the English architect Edward Cresy.

**OPPOSITE TOP LEFT** *The Ceremony in the Expiatory Chapel* (29 rue Pasquier, 8th arrondissement) by Lancelot-Théodore Turpin de Crissé (1782–1859), 1835. During the restoration of the monarchy in July, a mass was celebrated in memory of Louis XVI and Marie-Antoinette. In the centre, in the apse, is a group sculpture representing Marie-Antoinette supported by her faith. The work was begun by Lemot and finished by Cortot.

**LEFT** A general view of the theatres in the Boulevard du Temple before it was broken up by the Boulevard du Prince Eugène (now the Boulevard Voltaire) in 1862, by Martial Adolphe Potémont (1828–83). This part of the Boulevard du Temple was nicknamed the "Boulevard of Crime". On the far left is the Lyric Theatre (the old Historic Theatre of Alexandre Dumas) decorated with cariatids. Moving right, there is the Imperial Theatre with the large eagle on the top, then the Théâtre des Folies dramatiques and the Gaiety Theatre. To the right, is the Théâtre des Funambules with a portrait of the mime Jean-Baptiste Deburau on the front.

**ABOVE** The Galerie Véro-Dodat (1st arrondissement). Two charcutiers, Véro and Dodat had this arcade, which comprises 38 shops, built in 1826. It links rue Croix des Petits-Champs and rue Jean-Jacques Rousseau.

Many theatres were established on Boulevard du Temple, ranging from numbers 42 to 48 to the centre of the Place de la République. It was nicknamed the "Boulevard du Crime" because the plays put on there mainly dealt with murders, poisonings and assassinations. In 1823, Frédérick Lemaître (1800–76) enjoyed huge success in his role as the bandit Robert Macaire in the play *L'Auberge des Adrets* at the Théâtre de l'Ambigu-Comique, and mime artist Jean-Gaspard Deburau triumphed as Pierrot in the Théâtre des Funambules. From 1847 to 1850 Alexandre Dumas set up his own hall, the Théâtre Historique (which later became the Théâtre Lyrique). Under the Second Empire, the French prefect of the Seine, Baron Haussmann, knocked down the section of Boulevard du Temple where the theatres were located in order to develop Place de la République and the start of Boulevard Voltaire. However, on the odd-numbered side of the boulevard, one hall has survived to this day: Théâtre Déjazet, at 41 Boulevard du Temple in the 3rd arrondissement, because it was situated outside the perimeter of the major works.

In the wake of elections that favoured the opposition, Charles X passed four ordinances on 26 July 1830, which meant that the freedom of the press was suspended and publications (newspapers and pamphlets) had to be passed by the censor; the Chamber of Deputies was dissolved before it had even sat; the electoral law was changed to favour the votes of landowners; and new elections were scheduled for September. This legislation led to an uprising in Paris during 28–30 July, known as the Three Glorious Days, which ended in Charles X signing a withdrawal of the ordinances on 30 July 1830. Nevertheless, he was forced to abdicate on 2 August and fled into exile in England on 16 August. Power was conferred on the Duke of Orléans, who reigned as Louis-Philippe.

**ABOVE** The Pasha of Egypt, Mehmet Ali, offered Charles X a giraffe in 1826. Hoards of Parisians came to see the animal at the Jardin des Plantes.

**BELOW** Charles X distributes rewards to the artists at the end of the Salon of 1824 in the Louvre, painted by François Joseph Heim (1787–1865). The king is in the Salon carré, surrounded by the Director of Fine Arts, Vicomte de la Rochefoucauld, and the Director of Museums, Comte de Forbin.

**BELOW** *Fighting at the Porte Saint-Denis on 28 July 1830*, painted by Hippolyte Lecomte (1781–1857). There were a number of encounters between the insurgents and the royal troops on the grand boulevards. At the top of the Porte Saint-Denis (at the corner of the Boulevard de and the rue de la Faubourg Saint-Denis) an insurgent is waving the tricoleur flag, while others throw stones at the soldiers.

# Louis-Philippe

Louis-Philippe (1773–1850), who came from the younger branch of the Bourbon dynasty, was a descendant of Philippe d'Orléans, the brother of Louis XIV. In 1809, he married Marie-Amélie de Bourbon. Following the role that he played during the Revolution, Louis-Philippe lived in exile for 20 years, before finally returning to France in 1817. With his rank, huge fortune and Palais-Royal residence restored to him, the Duke of Orléans assumed the role of spokesperson for the liberal opposition. After securing a favourable vote in the Chamber of Deputies and Chamber of Peers, he swore the oath to the constitutional Charter and on 7 August 1830 he became Louis-Philippe I, the King of the French.

Rambuteau, the prefect of Paris, made improvements to public works and the road network in order to allow the million inhabitants to travel more easily around the city. He commissioned eight suspension bridges, established rues Rambuteau, de la Bourse and du Pont Louis-Philippe, and created many new pavements. The advent of the railways in 1828 could be seen in the construction of Gares Saint-Lazare (1837), Montparnasse and d'Austerlitz (1840), du Nord (1846), de l'Est and de Lyon (1849).

**OPPOSITE** King Louis-Philippe I, King of the French, takes the oath of the Charter in this painting by François Gérard from 1834.

**LEFT** An advertisement for a warehouse for Eau de Cologne by Pierre Jean Marie Farina, dating from the first half of nineteenth century. Jean Marie Farina (1685–1766), an Italian by birth, invented a perfume in 1709 which he called Eau de Cologne, as a token of appreciation for his adoptive city. Farina's Eau de Cologne was very popular in France.

**OPPOSITE ABOVE** The railway, shown in an engraving on coloured wood from c. 1848. The first railway line was opened between Paris and Saint-Germain and inaugurated, because of the dangers, by Queen Amélie on 24 August 1837.

**OPPOSITE BELOW** A lithograph by P. Benoist and J. Jacottet of the Church of la Madeleine.

In 1830, Louis-Philippe restored its civic function to the Pantheon, which had been reserved for religious worship since 1821. David d'Angers produced *La Patrie couronnant les hommes célèbres* (*The Homeland Crowning Famous Men*) on the pediment relief. The king also completed monuments, which had been left as building sites in the wake of the previous regime.

The Church of la Madeleine was started in 1755 and consecrated in 1845. The church was designed along the lines of a Classical temple, resting on a majestic plinth and surrounded by 52 Corinthian columns. Its basilica layout was chosen by Napoléon and executed by Pierre Vignon and then Jean-Jacques Huvé. The pediment relief completed by Philippe-Henri Lemaire in 1833 features *La Madeleine aux pieds du Christ lors du Jugement dernier* (*Mary Magdalene at Christ's Feet at the Last Judgement*). The fallen woman symbolized a saddened France in accordance with Louis XVIII's wishes. The lavish interior dedicated to Saint Mary has surprising elements, including a single nave and three domes borrowed from the architecture of Roman thermal baths.

**OPPOSITE ABOVE**  A view of the Place de la Bastille by Alphonse Testard, 1840. The Colonne de Juillet (July Column) is topped by the Spirit of Liberty holding the "flame of civilization" in her right hand and the broken chain of despotism in her left.

**OPPOSITE BELOW**  *The Return of Napoléon's Ashes in the Place de l'Etoile* by Théodore Jung. The funeral procession had a profound impact as it passed by.

**BELOW**  *The Fire at the Château d'Eau, Place du Palais-Royal, 24 February 1848*, by Eugène-Henri-Adolphe Hagnauer. The barricades multiplied, and the barracks and 18 court carriages were burnt. The following day, Louis-Philippe abdicated.

On the north side of Place de la Concorde, this church stands opposite the Palais-Bourbon at the south end of the square. In 1806 there was a proposal to harmonize the two buildings. Bernard Poyet gave the Palais-Bourbon a new façade, featuring a peristyle of twelve columns crowned with a pediment. Between 1837 and 1841, Pierre Cortot added the sculpture *La France appelant l'élite à la confection des lois* (*France Calling Upon Its Rulers to Make Laws*). In 1828, Jules de Joly began work on fitting out several function rooms, a wonderful library decorated by Eugène Delacroix, a spacious meeting chamber and a reception room.

On Place de la Bastille, which had lain empty since the demolition of the fortress, the king decided to erect the Colonne de Juillet (July Column) – a monument in honour of the citizens killed from 27 to 29 July 1830. Years earlier under the reign of Napoléon, Jean-Antoine Alavoine had planned a fountain, supplied with water from the l'Ourcq and decorated with an elephant, but by 1808 only the stone base had been built. Alavoine repurposed it as the base for the 50.5-m (165-ft) high, bronze column, topped by the "Spirit of Liberty" statue. On the column shaft, completed by Joseph-Louis Duc, the names of 504 heroes were inscribed: their spoils were buried in the underground gallery that had been provided under the fountain.

In 1840, Jacques-Ignace Hittorff restored the gardens of the Champs-Elysées, which had been ruined by Russian and English troops. He laid tarmac on the paths, and added fountains, pavilions and restaurants. He brightened up Place de la Concorde with the Fountain of the Rivers, a Maritime Fountain and female allegories representing the main cities in France; these were distributed around the Luxor Obelisk, erected in 1836. The square hosts splendid rostral columns with ships' prows – the symbol of Paris – containing gas lighting.

The Arc de Triomphe was inaugurated in 1836 and was decorated with hauts-reliefs – including *La Marseillaise*, François Rude's great masterpiece – glorifying the Republican armies as well as the Grande Armée (Great Army) of the Empire. Thirty major victories and the names of 150 battles and 660 French military heroes were carved into the wall of the arch: its full symbolic meaning was realized when Napoléon's ashes were returned on 15 December 1840.

The hearse, drawn by 16 horses decked in gold, passed under the Arc de Triomphe, down the Champs-Elysées and across Place de la Concorde before reaching the Church of Saint-Louis des Invalides. The Emperor's tomb found its place alongside Turenne's remains and Vauban's heart, which Napoleon had transferred to this sanctuary, turning it into a pantheon to the glorious military history of France.

The Eastern crisis of 1840 prompted Louis-Philippe to fortify the capital with the Thiers *enceinte*, a defensive ring 34 km (21 miles) long and 140 m (460 ft) wide, completed in 1846. Weakened by an economic crisis, the regime collapsed when Republicans demanding universal suffrage organized a series of fundraising meetings known as the "Banquets campaign", as a means of circumventing the ban on public assemblies. Demonstrations on 22 and 23 February 1848 triggered the uprising the following day, and the abdication of Louis-Philippe. The Republic was proclaimed on 25 February 1848.

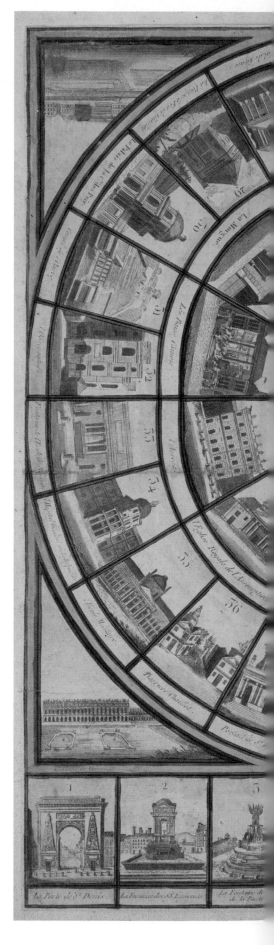

A game based on Parisian Monuments from circa 1820.

A variation of "The Game of the Goose", this game is made up of 63 squares and is played with two dice according to the following rules: the first player to reach square 63 – the Arc de Triomphe of the Tuileries Palace (Arc du Carrousel) – wins the game. Players must not land on the squares representing the customs gates (every ninth box).

A player who gets 9 in one throw of the dice, made up by 6 + 3, moves to square 26, the Hôtel de Ville. Throwing 9 with 5 + 4 takes a player to 53, in front of the statue of Henri IV on Pont-Neuf. Anyone landing on 6 – Pont des Arts – in the first throw has to pay the set price and go to square 12 to drown under the Pont du Jardin du Roi (now Pont d'Austerlitz). A player landing on square 19, Hôtel des Invalides, has to pay the set price and stay there while the other players each have two turns.

A player who lands on square 31 – Canal de l'Ourcq – stays there until another player releases him by taking his place.

If a player lands on square 42 – Hôtel-Dieu – he has to go back to square 30, to the Palais de la Chambre des Pairs (now the Senate, Palais du Luxembourg). Anyone landing on square 52 – the Sainte-Pélagie prison – stays there until released by another player.

A player landing on square 58 – the morgue – has to go right back to the beginning. The first player to be joined by a second player has to give up his position and go back to the second player's previous position.

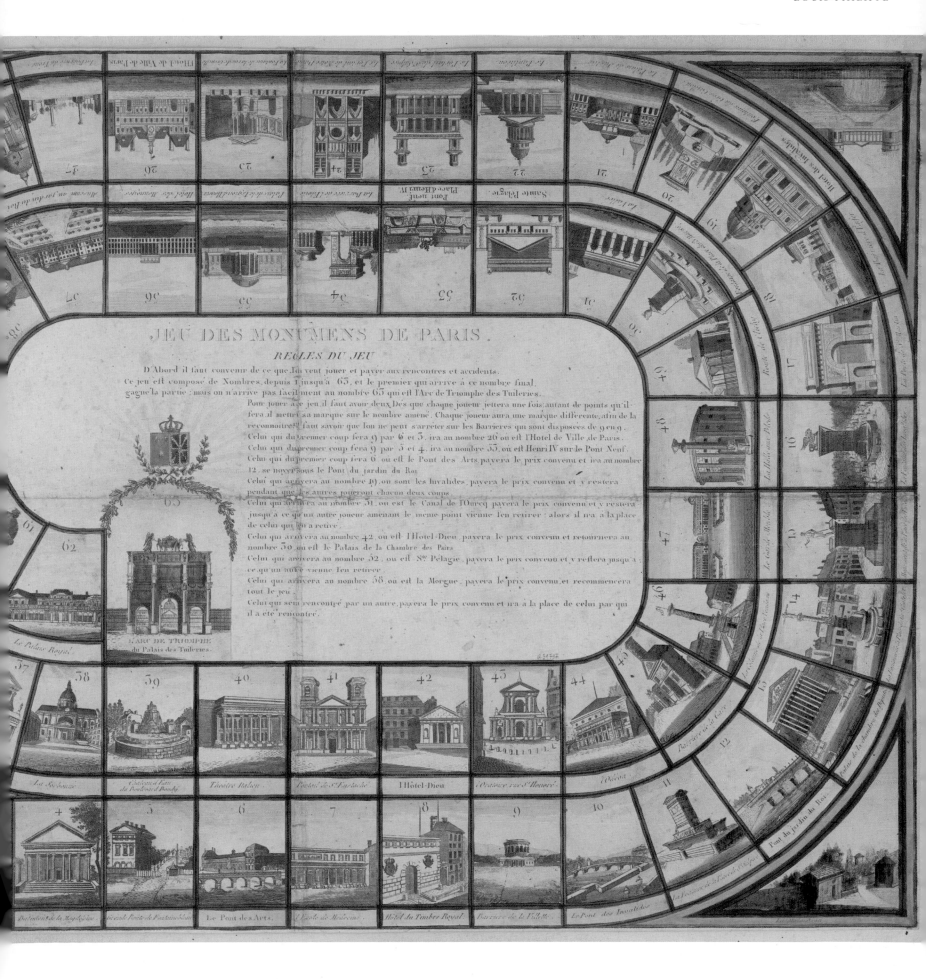

# "Le Grand Paris" of Napoléon III

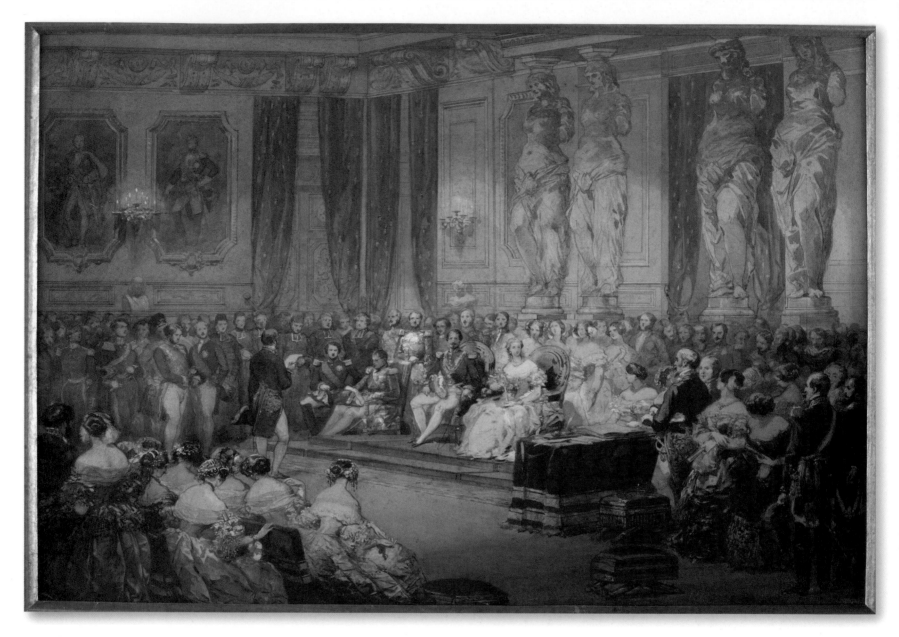

In the grip of an economic crisis, the provisional government of the Second Republic opened the National Workshops on 26 February 1848, with the aim of providing employment for around 15,000 workers. For the first time in France, on 23 April, a general election took place under universal suffrage, returning a large majority of Conservative deputies. Since they were unable to plan work for 120,000 unemployed people, these deputies closed the workshops on 20 June. The shutdown instigated violent hunger riots, which were brutally suppressed by General Louis–Eugène Cavaignac. Between 23 and 26 June, 4,000 insurgents and 1,600 military personnel were reported dead.

Charles Louis Napoléon Bonaparte – the 40-year-old third son of Louis Bonaparte and Hortense de Beauharnais – stood in the presidential elections under the banner of being the heir to Napoléon I, who was his uncle. He was elected to serve a four-year term by universal suffrage on 10 December 1848. The coup d'état

on 2 December 1851, which was ratified by a plebiscite on 21 December, extended his mandate to ten years. When the results of the 1852 referendum were declared, the "prince-president" Charles Louis was crowned Emperor Napoléon III, with 7,824,000 votes for and 253,000 against. In 1853, he married Eugénie de Montijo, who bore him a son, Eugène Louis Napoléon (1856–79).

In February 1852, the imperial couple moved into the Tuileries Palace, which speeded up Henri IV's project to connect the Louvre and the Tuileries Palace. Hector Lefuel executed the design by Louis Tullius Joachim Visconti, although he added an abundance of decoration that was Neo-Renaissance in style. However, shortly after its completion, the Tuileries Palace burned down on 24 May 1871. The intact foundations were levelled in 1883, permanently destroying the historical significance of this monumental edifice. The emperor's ceremonial suites survived.

Influenced by the ideas of Saint-Simon, Napoléon III saw

ABOVE A nineteenth-century watercolour of an official reception at the Tuileries by Eugène Lami. Napoléon III and the Empress Eugénie de Montijo (1826–1920) are shown in the Salon des Maréchaux that was situated in the Clock Pavilion, which no longer exists.

libre, aucun coin de son étroit foyer ne peut le défendre des regards étrangers. Quiconque passe a le droit de tourner le bouton de sa porte et de le forcer à répondre. Serviteur de cinquante volontés, il faut qu'il satisfasse à toutes. On lui demandera tour à tour compte des lettres reçues et de celles qu'on attend, des visiteurs accueillis ou renvoyés, des réclamations au propriétaire, des gênes du voisinage ; et s'il oublie, s'il se fatigue, un essaim de plaintes s'élève ! C'est le seul

(Dessin de M. Karl Girardet.)

habitant du logis auquel la négligence ou l'humeur ne soit jamais permise , et chacun de nous aurait assez de vertus s'il possédait la moitié de celles qu'il attend de son concierge.

Mais montons au premier étage avec ce valet qui porte un panier de vins dont il déguste les prémices. Ses deux confrères en livrée , qui attendent sur le palier, vont nous introduire dans la salle du bal. Que de lumière , de bruit et d'éclat ! à voir cette foule parée, qui ne croirait à sa joie! Et cepen-

LEFT  A cross-section view of a four-storey Parisian house, which was reproduced in *Magasin Pittoresque*, December 1847. On the ground floor in the concierge's lodge, the doorman is also working as a tailor. On the first floor, the ball is underway in a luxurious salon. On the second floor, a woman is watching over her sick child, while the father is composing tunes on his piano. The child's crying is interrupting his inspiration. On the third floor, a painter is surprised at the intrusion of a man into his studio. On the top floor, a female worker is sewing in her attic.

# RÉPUBLIQUE FRANÇAISE.

## Liberté, Egalité, Fraternité.

Conformément au Décret du Gouvernement provisoire de la République, du 25 Février 1848, par lequel il adopte les trois couleurs, disposées comme elles l'étaient pendant la République, le Délégué du Gouvernement provisoire au Département de la Police, ORDONNE à tous les Chefs des Monuments Publics, et, en leur absence, aux Concierges desdits Monuments, d'y arborer de suite un drapeau, de la plus grande dimension possible, portant les couleurs ainsi placées :

## Bleu, Rouge et Blanc ;

de telle sorte que, le BLEU tenant à la lance, le ROUGE soit au milieu et que le BLANC flotte.

Le Délégué de la République au Département de la Police,

Paris, le 27 Février 1848.
CAUSSIDIÈRE.

BOUCQUIN, Imprimeur du département de la Police, ruede la Sainte-Chapelle, 5. — Paris 1848.

ABOVE A decree by the Republic of France, of 25 February 1848, in which the provisional government adopts the three colours of the flag.

During the 1848 revolution, the insurgents flew the red flag over the Hôtel de Ville, signalling a break from the tricolour flag re-established under the reign of Louis-Philippe. However, Alphonse de Lamartine insisted on the tricolour flag, arguing that it "had been around the world with the Republic and the Empire, while the red flag had only been around the Champ de Mars in the blood of the people".

Legend created the tricolour emblem on 17 July 1789: Louis XVI met with Bailly, the Mayor of Paris, and General Lafayette. As a sign of reconciliation, the king tied a red and blue ribbon with the colours of the city to his hat, alongside the white cockade. The tricolour cockade was adopted from then on.

The public celebration of the three colours took place on the Champ de Mars during the Fête de la Fédération on 14 July 1790. The tricolour flag, designed by Jacques Louis David, became the national emblem in the decree of 1794. "The pavilion, like the national flag, will be made up of the three national colours arranged in three equal strips, in such a way that blue will be attached to the pavilion guard, white in the middle, and red flying."

RIGHT A coloured and decorated lithograph of souvenirs of the Exposition Universelle (World's Fair) of 1855 by Jules Chaste from the same year. Bronzes, crystals and gold artefacts were displayed in the hall of the Palais de l'Industrie.

**ABOVE** Victor-Gabriel Gilbert's 1880 painting of the Market Square of Les Halles. The traders had permanent stalls in the square which adjoined the cheviot of Saint- Eustache Church in the 1st arrondissement.

**RIGHT** The Grand Corner Salon in the apartment of Napoléon III, which was conceived by Lefuel and inaugurated in February 1861. Occupied by the Minister of Finance from 1871 to 1989, it is situated in the Louvre Museum overlooking the rue de Rivoli.

the economy as the engine of society. Supporting industry, agriculture and trade; improving productivity and carrying out large-scale public works were the means by which he intended to raise the living standards of ordinary citizens and achieve social transformation. He founded the Crédit Foncier, a national mortgage bank, which resulted in an extraordinary level of modernization across society.

The emperor revived the project to expand Les Halles market, which had been launched in 1848, and symbolically laid the foundation stone of a pavilion on 15 September 1851. Victor Baltard constructed ten pavilions in brick, iron, cast iron and glass, which were destroyed in 1971, despite numerous protests.

In 1851, Jacques Ignace Hittorff built the Cirque d'Hiver (Winter Circus). His use of the shape of a polygon with 20 sides allowed him to design an amphitheatre and a circulation gallery around the ring, with a capacity for 3,900 people. The zinc-covered wooden structure formed a light frame, with a painted ceiling in the style of a classical awning. The building's overall harmony, equestrian statues, rich interior decoration and vibrant colours – inspired by ancient Greek architecture – all contribute to the magic of the shows performed here.

In 1853, Napoléon III appointed Georges-Eugène Haussmann (1809–1891) – a meticulous and efficient administrator – as prefect of the Seine département. As well as planning the annexation of the suburban municipalities, Haussmann designed networks for improving the the sanitation of the city. In 1872, he organized networks of drinking water supplies and sewage drainage systems (600 km/373 miles in 1872). He also mapped out a framework of cambered roads, side pavements and gutters, which were suitable for street cleaning.

In 1855, Napoléon III organized the Exposition Universelle (World's Fair), which was attended by Queen Victoria. The panoramic rotunda brought together luxury objects made by the Baccarat, Sèvres and Gobelins manufactories to exhibit French artistic superiority. Five million visitors discovered the paintings of Ingres and Delacroix, as well as English watercolours, numbering 5,000 pictures in total, with provenances in 28 countries.

The railway network, which in 1870 stretched to 20,000 km (12,430 miles) and carried 110 million passengers and 45 million tonnes of goods over the year, was developed in tandem with building stations, widely seen as the new gates of Paris. The Gare du Nord was designed by Hittorff and constructed from 1861 to 1866. The architect combined a vast metal hall with stone façades, decorated with female allegories. These symbols represent Paris, Arras, Lille and Beauvais, as well as European capitals such as London, Vienna and Brussels.

At that time, the Wall of the Farmers-General, which was 3.3 m (11 ft) high, marked the boundary of Paris. The Thiers *enceinte* was built at a variable distance from this wall, ranging from 1 to 3 km (¾ to 1¾ miles). The structure divided municipalities such as Auteuil, but included others like Belleville, creating an unmanageable area: 364,000 inhabitants under 24 different municipalities were living squeezed between two walls.

Napoléon III introduced a decree on 3 November 1859 to absorb this territory outside the city's gates, up to the defensive ring. Passy, Auteuil, Batignolles-Monceau, Montmartre, La Chapelle, La Villette, Belleville, Charonne, Bercy, Vaugirard, Grenelle and 13 partial sections of municipalities were annexed. The Thiers *enceinte* marked the new boundaries of the city – "le Grand Paris" – which was divided into 20 arrondissements. In place of the demolished Wall of the Farmers-General, the ring of outer boulevards demarcated "le Vieux Paris" ("Old Paris").

**LEFT** The Cirque d'Hiver (Winter Circus), 110 rue Amelot, 11th arrondissement. Opened on 10 December 1852, the circus included acrobatic dancing, a flying trapeze and pantomime acts which were added to equestrian shows. The circus was run by the Bouglione family from 1934.

**BELOW** The Gare du Nord around 1850 is shown in this lithograph by Charles Rivière. The Gare du Nord (112 rue de Maubeuge, 10th arrondissement) is linked to the Gare de l'Est by the Boulevard de Magenta.

# Haussmann's Achievements

**H**aussmann used pioneering legal means to transform the city. He resorted without hesitation to applying the law on expropriation and secured a huge amount of funding through public loans. His priorities were to improve sanitation and to get the traffic moving more freely in the city.

The overpopulated city centre, which had 1,000 inhabitants per hectare on Île de la Cité and Place du Châtelet, was decimated by cholera epidemics in 1832, 1848 and 1853. This area was crammed with poor housing, blocking the route between the medieval Left Bank and the prosperous Right Bank, which was constantly expanding westwards.

Haussmann completely demolished the Île de la Cité, leaving only a few houses standing. He built the Hôtel-Dieu (main hospital), the Tribunal de Commerce (commercial court) and the Caserne de la Cité (municipal barracks), and laid out a huge square in front of Notre-Dame Cathedral. From there onwards, travel between the riverbanks was facilitated by the construction of new bridges and the Boulevard du Palais.

Concerned about the flow of traffic, Haussmann joined up Boulevard Sébastopol and Boulevard Saint-Michel, creating a north–south axis intersection at Place du Châtelet, with an east–west axis at the junction of rue de Rivoli and rue Saint-Paul. On the banks of the Seine, Place du Châtelet was remodelled around the Palmier Fountain, which in turn was recentred and embellished with four sphinxes. On either side of the square, Gabriel Davioud completed two theatres in 1862: the Théâtre de la Ville, where Sarah Bernhardt performed, and the Théâtre du Châtelet, which played host to magical performances.

On the Left Bank, where it opens out at Pont Saint-Michel, the square of the same name is framed by a number of harmonious buildings. Gabriel Davioud's St Michael Fountain, which depicts the saint wrestling with the devil, occupies the central niche of a triumphal arch decorated with a profusion of sculptures. Boulevard Saint-Germain, alternately straight and winding, follows the slope of St Geneviève's Hill. The avenue acts as a supply route to the different quarters of the Left Bank.

The boulevards and avenues linking the key service points in the city – stations, barracks, town halls, markets, schools, hospitals and parks – are characterized by their extensive width and layout at roundabouts, such as Places de l'Etoile, de l'Alma and Voltaire. Keen to open up the peripheral arrondissements to the east, Haussmann planned a long through-route, consisting of Avenue Simon Bolivar, rue des Pyrénées and Avenue Michel Bizot.

Davioud completed large-scale works from 1862 onwards. He laid out gardens on the Boulevard Richard-Lenoir that covered Canal Saint-Martin, which had been lowered by 5.5 m (18 ft). He transformed Place de la République, prettifying it with lion-shaped fountains, and giving it a monumental appearance with the construction of the Magasins Réunis department store opposite the Vérines Barracks, dating from 1859.

Districts were ripped apart by 90 km (56 miles) of new roads, involving the demolition of 20,000 houses and the rebuilding of 43,700 new residences with restrictions on their height, roofs, windows and balconies. The residents of the squalid districts were cast out to

**OPPOSITE ABOVE** An engraving by Félix Thorigny of the new Fountain of Saint-Michel on the Boulevard de Sébastopol Saint-Michel (6th arrondissement, on the Left Bank), which was unveiled on 15 August 1860. The fountain backs onto the building which separates the rue Danton (to the right) from the Boulevard Saint-Michel (on the left).

**OPPOSITE BELOW** The Pont au Change links the Palais de Justice and the Conciergerie, on the Île de la Cité, and the Place du Châtelet. It is ornamented by the Palmier Fountain and overlooked by the Théâtre du Châtelet (Châtelet Theatre).

**BELOW** A view of the Church of Saint-Augustin, Place Saint-Augustin, 8th arrondissement. It is thought that the crypt was due to house the mausoleum of Napoléon III and his family.

the industrial zones in the east. However, Napoleon III did allocate funds for the construction of workers' housing, as seen at 58 rue Rochechouart and 64 Boulevard Diderot.

Following traditional planning tenets, Haussmann drew straight axes culminating in a monument – Boulevard de Sébastopol ends in Gare de l'Est, for instance – and highlighted buildings with a wide road, such as rue Victoria leading to the Hôtel de Ville. To cover up the bend in Boulevard Malesherbes, Victor Baltard built the Saint-Augustin Church in 1860. The building's stone-cased iron structure, 80 m (262 ft) high dome and eclectic style combined to make this monument the flagship of this new residential area.

In 1862, Napoleon III sealed the Avenue de l'Opéra by commissioning an outstanding lyric theatre, and surrounding buildings designed in the Corinthian order. The Opéra, by Charles Garnier, exudes a richly elegant decorative style, thanks to the use of different stones, marbles and granite, in colours matching the mosaics and bronzes.

The construction of Avenue Foch linked Paris to the Bois de Boulogne, which was fashioned in the English style by Jean-Charles Alphand. Winding paths, water features, restaurants and the Zoological Gardens enjoyed such a level of success that Napoléon III asked Alphand to remodel the Bois de Vincennes. The public realm was transformed by green spaces, including the Monceau, Montsouris and Buttes Chaumont parks, as well as 24 squares, tree-lined avenues, fountains, kiosks, advertising columns and street lamps.

The Exposition Universelle (World's Fair) of 1867 attracted 15 million visitors, who were eager to explore a giant palace with themed galleries, which offered food, everyday objects, clothing, furniture, works of art and industrial objects. This retrospective exhibition marked the pinnacle of the emperor's reign, which came to a tragic end three years later with the outbreak of the Franco-Prussian War.

The defeat at Sedan and capture of Napoléon III on 20 September 1870 instigated the collapse of the Second Empire. The deposed emperor went into exile in Chislehurst, Kent, where he died on 9 January 1873. Although these dramatic events overshadowed the remarkable works of Napoléon III, the magnificent city improvements carried out by Haussmann under the emperor's surveillance shaped most of Paris's identity as it stands today.

**ABOVE** The Emperor and Empress are shown skating in the Bois de Boulogne in this 1862 painting by Johann Mongels Culverhouse.

**OPPOSITE** Jean-Baptiste Detaille's 1878 painting of the opening of the Paris Opèra on 5 January 1875. The architect Charles Garnier welcomes the Lord Mayor of London. The balconies overhang the large double staircase, allowing the spectators to indulge in social gossip.

# Vibrant Paris – 1800–70

Paris, a capital city owing its dynamic energy to shops, theatres, restaurants and cafés, enjoyed a rich intellectual and artistic life as the nineteenth century progressed. Shops filled up with new clothes sold for fixed prices, and offered free entrance, with no obligation to buy any goods.

From 1800 until 1850, these shops proliferated in the city. They included Au Grand Colbert at 2 rue Vivienne in the 2nd arrondissement, À la Ville de Paris at 170 rue Montmartre in the 2nd arrondissement and Au Siège de Corinthe, named after a Rossini opera, at 52 rue de la Chaussée d'Antin in the 9th arrondissement, and they offered different types of seasonal fabrics for clothing, haberdashery and household materials. During the Second Empire, department stores started to emerge, which were described by Émile Zola as "cathedrals of modern commerce". In 1852, Aristide Boucicaut joined Justin Videau in founding Le Bon Marché at 22 rue de Sèvres in the 7th arrondissement, the shop that gave Zola inspiration for the novel *The Ladies' Delight*.

Along the Grands Boulevards, cafés opened late into the evening, attracting a wide range of customers. Café Hardy (later known as La Maison Dorée), situated at 20 Boulevard des Italiens in the 9th arrondissement, was popular with Alexander Dumas, the brothers Edmond and Jules de Goncourt, and Jacques Offenbach. Café Tortoni at 22 Boulevard des Italiens was renowned for its sorbets. The café benefited from its location opposite the Théâtre Italien, on the site of the Opéra Comique, at Place Boieldieu in the 2nd arrondissement, where opera lovers applauded the performance of Gioachino Rossini's *The Italian Girl* in Algiers in 1817 and *The Barber of Seville* in 1819.

Gioachino Rossini (1792–1868) was musical director of the Théâtre Italien from 1824 to 1826, where he composed the operas *William Tell* and *The Journey to Reims* on the occasion of Charles X's coronation. Jacques Offenbach (1819–80) performed *Parisian Life* in 1866 at the Théâtre du Palais-Royal, situated at 38 rue Montpensier in the 1st arrondissement. The last act of this operetta takes place in the Café Anglais at 13 Boulevard des Italiens in the 2nd arrondissement, which opened in 1802 and was frequented by Balzac and Flaubert. Offenbach enjoyed huge success at the Théâtre des Variétés at 7 Boulevard Montmartre in the 2nd arrondissement, with *The Beautiful Helen* and *The Grand Duchess of Gerolstein*, which were performed by the soprano Hortense Schneider.

Paris is fortunate enough to have several museums dedicated to famous nineteenth-century writers and painters. These include

**RIGHT** A coloured engraving by Eugène-Charles-François Guérard (1821–66) of the Café Tortoni on Boulevard des Italiens at 4.00 pm. Situated on the right, the Café Tortoni had a terrace at the corner of 22 Boulevard des Italiens and 2 rue Taitbout in the 9th arrondissement.

**BELOW** An engraving by Charles Walter and de Thierry of the opening on 3 April 1843 of new departments in the Magasins de la Ville de Paris, which was situated at 174 rue Montmartre. This fashion shop, founded in 1841 by Prosper, Deschamps & Collinet, closed in 1882.

the houses of Victor Hugo and Balzac, the Museum of Romantic Life and the Eugène Delacroix Museum. The Museum of Victor Hugo (1802–85) is based in the townhouse at 6 Place des Vosges in the 4th arrondissement, where the novelist rented the second-floor apartment from 1832 to 1848. The building houses furniture, mementos, manuscripts and fine drawings, created by the writer throughout his life.

Hugo established his leadership of the Romantic movement with his drama *Hernani*. The premiere on 25 February 1830 ranked as one of the great scandals in theatre history: it was nicknamed the "Battle of Hernani" because of the conflicting responses that it provoked from audience members. In the apartment that houses his museum, Hugo wrote the plays *Lucrèce Borgia*, *Marie Tudor*, *Ruy Blas*, as well as the poems "Interior Voices", "Beams and Shadows" and "Return of the Ashes". From 1845 to 1847, he worked on the first draft of *Les Misérables*. When Charles Louis Napoléon Bonaparte's *coup d'état* took place on 2 December 1851, the writer chose to go into exile. In 1856, Hugo purchased Hauteville House in Guernsey, where he spent his exile, and he did not return to Paris until 5 September 1870, after the fall of the Second Empire.

Honoré de Balzac (1799–1850) took refuge at 7 rue Raynouard in the 16th arrondissement from 1840 until 1847. There he occupied a five-room apartment with a garden and lived under the pseudonym of Monsieur de Breugnol, which was a version of his housekeeper's name, Louise Breugnot. To appease his creditors he sold his house, the Maison des Jardies in Sèvres, at auction. As a precautionary measure, he was assigned a password to gain access to his house. The apartment had a second entrance on 24 rue Berton, which allowed the writer to come and go with complete peace of mind. While living here, Balzac wrote the novels *The Black Sheep*, *The Splendours and Miseries of Courtesans* and *Cousin Bette*.

The Museum of Romantic Life at 16 rue Chaptal in the 9th arrondissement displays the paintings of Ary Scheffer (1795–1848), who lived in this house from 1830 until he died. Scheffer was known for his hospitality, in welcoming artists such as Rossini, Liszt and Chopin to gather at his home. He also invited the novelist George Sand (1804–76) to visit. Today, the museum displays artworks, furniture and jewellery that belonged to the author.

Eugène Delacroix (1798–1863) lived in an apartment with a studio at 6 rue de Furstenberg in the 6th arrondissement from 1857 until his death. This residence now houses the Eugène Delacroix Museum to commemorate the painter. Earlier, Delacroix had left his lodgings at 54 rue Notre-Dame-de-Lorette to be closer to Saint-Sulpice Church, where he had been working on the decoration of the Chapel of the Angels since 1847. Weakened by illness, he wanted to avoid a long journey so that he could channel his energies into completing this remarkable decorative work, which he finally did in 1861.

**PREVIOUS PAGES** An aerial view of the Place des Vosges in the 3rd and 4th arrondissements). The garden, bordered by *hôtels particuliers* (grand town houses) from the seventeenth century, was modified in the nineteenth century and ornamented by four fountains designed in 1829 by François-Julien Ménager.

**OPPOSITE** Victor Hugo's bedroom at the Maison de Victor Hugo (6 Place des Vosges, 4th arrondissement). This is the bedroom of the apartment where Victor Hugo lived from 1881 until his death in 1885 at 124 Avenue Victor Hugo (in the 16th arrondissement) which has been reconstructed at the Maison de Victor Hugo.

**ABOVE** A poster by Jules Chéret (1836–1932) advertising *La Vie Parisienne*, a comic opera with words by Henri Meilhac and Ludovic Halévy and music by Jacques Offenbach, in 1866.

**RIGHT** Honoré de Balzac's study in the Maison de Balzac (24 rue Raynouard, 16th arrondissement). The room is furnished with a walnut table and a Louis XIII armchair.

# The Paris Commune

After the Republic was declared in the Hôtel de Ville (City Hall) on 4 September 1870, General Trochu presided over the Government of National Defence.

Paris was surrounded by the Prussians (as a result of their invasion of France) on 19 September, and fell under siege until early the next year. The capital was bombarded, for the city's defensive wall could no longer protect its population from the fire of cannons located 8 km (5 miles) away.

The Parisians lived through a harsh autumn and winter, when neither wood nor coal was available for heating. As supplies could no longer be guaranteed, foodstuffs such as wheat and meat ran out. People were forced to eat horsemeat, then dogs, cats and even rats. The animals in the Zoological Gardens, including elephants, zebras, buffalo and bears, were also killed for food.

On 18 January 1871, King Wilhelm I of Prussia managed to unite the German states and was proclaimed their Emperor in the Hall of Mirrors at the Château de Versailles. The following day, General Trochu led 100,000 men in an attempt to breach the blockade, but failed at Buzenval, where 5,000 soldiers perished.

**BELOW** A painting by Jules Didier (1831–92) and Jacques Guiaud (1811–76) of the proclamation of the fall of the Empire on 4 September 1870, made on the steps of the Palais du Corps Législatif (the seat of the National Assembly) after its last sitting by Jules Favre and Léon Gambetta.

**OPPOSITE ABOVE** A painting by Jules Didier (1831–92) and Jacques Guiaud (1811–76) of the messages carried by pigeons being viewed. Each pigeon carried hundreds of messages between a besieged Paris and the provinces. The despatches were reduced to microscopic size by photograph. On their arrival, they were projected onto a screen to be deciphered.

**OPPOSITE BELOW** The queue at an épicerie in November 1870, painted by Alfred Decaen (born 1820) and Jacques Guiaud (1811–76). The épicerie Félix Potin was at the corner of 51 rue Réaumur and 99 Boulevard de Sébastopol (2nd arrondissement). The National Guard can be seen in training in the road.

**OVERLEAF** The cannon of the National Guard are depicted in 1871 at the top of Montmartre Hill with its windmills in this nineteenth-century colour drawing by Dupendant. Thiers attempted to recover them on 18 March 1871 with the help of the army.

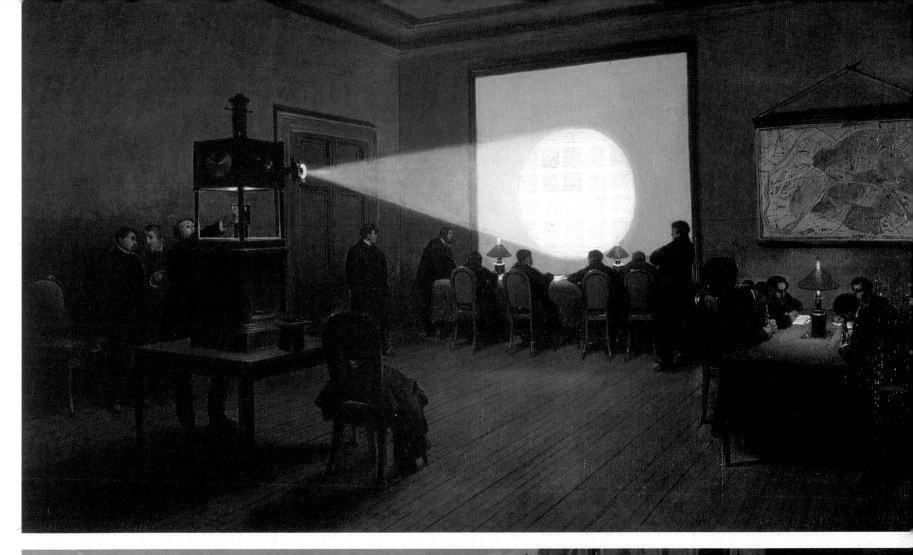

Following the National Assembly elections, the deputies sitting at Bordeaux decided to sign the armistice on 12 February. Five days later, they appointed Adolphe Thiers as Head of the Executive Power of the French Republic.

On 26 February, Thiers and Jules Favre (Minister of Foreign Affairs) signed the preliminary peace accord at Versailles, which was ratified on 10 May in the Treaty of Frankfurt. The conditions imposed by the German Chancellor, Otto von Bismarck, were draconian: he called for payment within three years of five billion gold francs in reparations, the transfer of Alsace and North Lorraine, and the withdrawal of French troops to the south of the Loire. Parisians felt that this capitulation was a betrayal.

On 1 March 1871, the German army marched symbolically down the Champs-Élysées before evacuating the capital. On 10 March, the government withdrew to Versailles, leaving the National Guard (a citizens' militia) behind, as the only armed force in Paris. With the intention of disarming the capital, Thiers sent troops under the command of Generals Lecomte and Thomas on 18 March to retake the 200 cannon, which the National Guard had secured at Montmartre and Belleville. While the Versailles troops were agreeing on terms with the Parisians, the National Guard executed the two generals. The central committee of the National Guard then occupied the Hôtel de Ville, and established the Paris Commune, a government that briefly ruled the city from 28 March until 28 May.

However, during the course of the week from 21 to 28 May, the government suppressed the Paris Commune. Troops from Versailles entered the city on 21 May by Porte de Saint-Cloud in the 16th arrondissement. The Communards set fire to many monuments: the Court of Audit and the Finance Ministry on 23 May, and the Tuileries Palace and Hôtel de Ville the next day. Summary

**BELOW** A panoramic view of the fires which set Paris alight on the 23, 24 and 25 May 1871, part of a lithograph by Émile Deroy.

executions were carried out on both sides. On 24 May, the Archbishop of Paris, Monseigneur Darboy, and five other hostages were executed by the Communards in La Grande Roquette Prison at 166 rue de la Roquette in the 11th arrondissement.

On 26 May, the Communards killed 48 hostages, including priests and policemen, in what became known as the "hostages villa", at 85 rue Haxo in the 20th arrondissement. Two days later, 147 Communards were defeated by government troops in front of the Communards' Wall in Père-Lachaise Cemetery. The "blood-soaked week" claimed around 20,000 victims, while 43,000 people were arrested.

The Sacré Coeur Basilica at 35 rue du Chevalier de La Barre in the 18th arrondissement was completed on the initiative of two prominent citizens, Alexandre Legentil and Hubert Rohault de Fleury, who vowed to build a basilica in expiation for the Franco-Prussian War and the Paris Commune. The project sparked off fierce debate, especially on the part of Émile Zola. The funding of the basilica was guaranteed by private donations. The Archbishop of Paris, Monseigneur Guibert, offered a plot of land for the Sacré Coeur on Montmartre Hill, the site of St Denis's martyrdom, as well as confrontations during the Paris Commune. In 1876, the architect Paul Abadie (1812–84) started construction work on the Sacré Coeur, which was carried out by five architects: Honoré Daumet, Charles J. Laisné, Henri Rauline, Lucien Magne and Louis-Jean Hulot. The church was designed in a Neo-Byzantian style and inaugurated on 19 November 1886: the cladding was made of stone from Souppes-sur-Loing, giving it a shimmering white appearance.

**ABOVE** The Basilica of the Sacré-Coeur, 35 rue du Chevalier de La Barre in the 18th arrondissement. The building, which was only completed in 1919, was topped by a dome 83.33 m (273½ ft) high and a bell tower that is 84 m (275 ft) tall, which contains a bell nicknamed "la Savoyarde".

**RIGHT** A portrait of Sir Richard Wallace.

# THE WALLACE FOUNTAINS

Sir Richard Wallace (1818–90) inherited the Château de Bagatelle in 1870, along with works of art collected by his father, Lord Hertford, which were later brought together as the Wallace Collection in London. When he was staying in Paris during 1870–71, Wallace donated part of his fortune to pay for military ambulances, distribute food tokens in town halls and fuel for the poor. In return for his generosity, Thiers awarded him the Cross of Commander of the Legion of Honour and Queen Victoria made him a baronet. On noticing that the lack of a water supply had been critical during the siege, Wallace funded the construction of 40 drinking fountains in 1871. Charles Auguste Lebourg sculpted these fountains.

# The Age of Impressionism

The first president of the Third Republic, Adolphe Thiers, was elected by the Senate and Chamber of Deputies, which came together in the National Assembly on 31 August 1871. By floating two loans, he managed to pay the war indemnity of five billion gold francs, anticipating the withdrawal of Prussian occupation troops on 16 September 1873. However, during that year, the conservative majority favoured Marshal de Mac-Mahon, who planned to restore the monarchy in the person of the Comte de Chambord (Charles X's grandson).

In 1878, Mac-Mahon invited 36 nations to attend the Exposition Universelle (World's Fair), but left out the German and Ottoman empires. The structure of the Palais du Trocadéro, built in a Moorish style by Gabriel Davioud, is all that remains of this temporary exhibition. Mac-Mahon came up against the Republican majority and resigned in 1879.

The victory of the Republicans over the Royalists was confirmed in 1879, with the election of President Jules Grévy. Attached to the symbols that legitimized the Republic, the deputies left Versailles and re-established the seat of the National Assembly in the Palais-Bourbon. "La Marseillaise", composed by Rouget de Lisle, which had been decreed the official song of France on 14 July 1795 was confirmed as the official national anthem.

The day of 14 July was designated a public holiday, to mark the storming of the Bastille in 1789 and the Fête de la Fédération in 1790. The annual celebration was intended to be a demonstration of national unity. This was made law in June 1880 and linked to the general amnesty for the events of the Paris Commune.

The festival of 14 July 1880 on Place de la République gathered around a temporary statue, an allegory of the

**BELOW** Alfred Roll's painting of 14 July 1880 (from the same year). The first celebration was on the Place de la République. The enthusiastic public are seen converging on the President, Sadi Carnot, and other illustrious persons, such as Massenet and Zola.

Republic executed in plaster by Léopold and Charles Morice. The permanent monument, completed in 1883, was composed of a high base, decorated with 12 bas-reliefs and embellished with allegorical figures: Liberty, Equality and Fraternity. The lion crouching beside the ballot box symbolizes the power of universal suffrage. This pedestal supports the bronze figure of La République, who is crowned with a laurel wreath and a phyrigian hat, wears a classical toga and holds out an olive branch of peace.

The Hôtel de Ville, which burned down in 1871, was replaced by a more spacious building designed by the architects Théodore Ballu, Édouard Deperthes and Jean-Camille Formigé. Although they replicated the Renaissance façade of Dominique de Cortone, they introduced many statues and an interior layout for official receptions. This confirmed the prestigious role of the Hôtel de Ville, which was inaugurated on 13 July 1883. The lavish decoration of the salons, completed in 1887, features historical events, street scenes and landscapes.

Government ministers Léon Gambetta and Jules Ferry reinforced the Republican values of the regime by advocating secular education for all. Primary school was made obligatory in a law passed on 28 March 1882, while the following year a new law enabled the opening of the first secondary school for girls, the Lycée Fénelon in the 6th arrondissement.

Public buildings such as town halls and universities glorified the tradition of democracy that stemmed from the events of 1789 with painted decorations funded by the State. For instance, Pierre Puvis de Chavannes created a fresco, *The Sacred Wood of Arts and Sciences*, in the large hall of the new Sorbonne, which was rebuilt by Henri-Paul Nénot from 1885 to 1901.

**ABOVE** An admission ticket for the Jardin Zoologique d'Acclimatation in the Bois de Boulogne, from 1882. Napoleon III, accompanied by Empress Eugénie, inaugurated the Jardin Zoologique d'Acclimatation (zoo and acclimatization gardens on the Avenue du Mahatma Gandhi, 16th arrondissement) on 6 October 1860. The gardens were the brainchild of the scholar Isidore Geoffroy Saint-Hilaire, President of the Imperial Foundation for Zoological Acclimatization. On show were a huge variety of plants (such as banana trees, redwoods and bamboos) and animals originating from every country, such as orang-utans, zebus, wildebeest and hippopotami. Nowadays, the gardens are devoted to botany, as well as being home to an amusement park.

# THE EIFFEL TOWER

The Eiffel Tower was built as a spectacular marker to the exhibition entrance, but proved to be an aesthetic and technical challenge. From 26 January 1887 to 31 March 1889, around 250 workers assembled more than 18,000 metal pieces with rivets in the Eiffel factories, creating a gigantic meccano structure. Criticized in a public protest by 47 of the leading artists of the time, the Eiffel Tower is actually seen as a hymn of praise to technical progress. The 325-m (1066-ft) high Eiffel Tower stands today as an enduring symbol of Paris.

**ABOVE** Claude Monet's 1873 painting of the carnival in the Boulevard des Capucines.

**RIGHT** Paul Delance's 1889 painting entitled *The Eiffel Tower and the Champ de Mars in January 1889: Work on the Exposition Universelle*.

**OPPOSITE ABOVE** *A View of the Saint-Martin Canal*, painted by Alfred Sisley in 1870. The painter seized on the reverberations of the light from the cloudy sky on the calm water of the canal.

**OPPOSITE BELOW** Théobald Chartran's 1904 painting of the celebrations at the Panthéon to commemorate the centenary of the birth of Victor Hugo in the presence of President Félix Emile Loubet on 26 February 1902.

Alongside this academic painting style, esteemed by official Salons of the time, 30 artists organized an independent exhibition, without a judging panel, at the Boulevard des Capucines in 1874. One of the 165 canvases on show, *Impression, Sunrise* by Claude Monet, was derided by a journalist for being "impressionistic". However, the name stuck to the community of artists with whom he associated, including Paul Cézanne, Gustave Caillebotte, Edgar Degas, Claude Monet, Camille Pissarro, Auguste Renoir and Alfred Sisley, as they went on to exhibit in seven group shows between 1876 and 1886. These Impressionists, together with other painters such as Édouard Manet and Vincent van Gogh, aimed to capture immediate visual impressions of light and colour by adopting a fresh pictorial approach in their practice. They depicted acquaintances and everyday subjects using fragmented brushstrokes and applied thick layers of paint to blank canvases.

The state funeral of Victor Hugo and his entombment in the Panthéon took place on 1 June 1885. On this occasion, the building regained its civilian function once and for all. Works by Laurent Marqueste and Jean Antoine Injalbert in the Panthéon honour the heroes of the Republic.

Following the resignation of Jules Grévy, Sadi Carnot was elected President in 1887. He made plans for the Exposition Universelle (World's Fair) to be held from 5 May to 31 October 1889, commemorating the centenary of the French Revolution. The opening ceremony on 5 May celebrated the inauguration of the Estates General in 1789. On the flag-decorated Place de la Nation, a plaster model of Jules Dalou's sculptural work, *Triumph of the Republic*, was erected on 21 September 1889, the anniversary of the foundation of the Republic.

PARENT & Cie, Paris-Bruxelles.

VUE PANORAMIQUE DE

RIGHT A poster for the 1889 International Exhibition in Paris. This panoramic view is oriented west to east. On the Left Bank, the Eiffel Tower takes up the northernmost part of the Champ de Mars beside the Seine. On the tower's axis, flower beds with a bright ornamental fountain in the middle separate the Palace of Fine Arts (to the east) – dedicated to painting and sculpture – from the Palace of the Liberal Arts (to the west), housing the retrospective on work and the anthropological sciences.

The entrance to the U-shaped Palace of Diverse Industries is through a central dome overlooking the gardens and the Pavilions of the City of Paris. The Gallery of Machines is located at the far end of the Champ de Mars. A large number of pavilions are spread around the bottom of the Eiffel Tower.

On the Right Bank, the Trocadero Palace, built in 1878, houses the ethnographic museum and the festival hall set up in the rotunda. The gardens are organized completely around the exhibition of horticultural products, notably the Japanese bonsais. The pavilions devoted to the colonies are lined up on the Invalides esplanade, between Quai d'Orsay and rue de Grenelle.

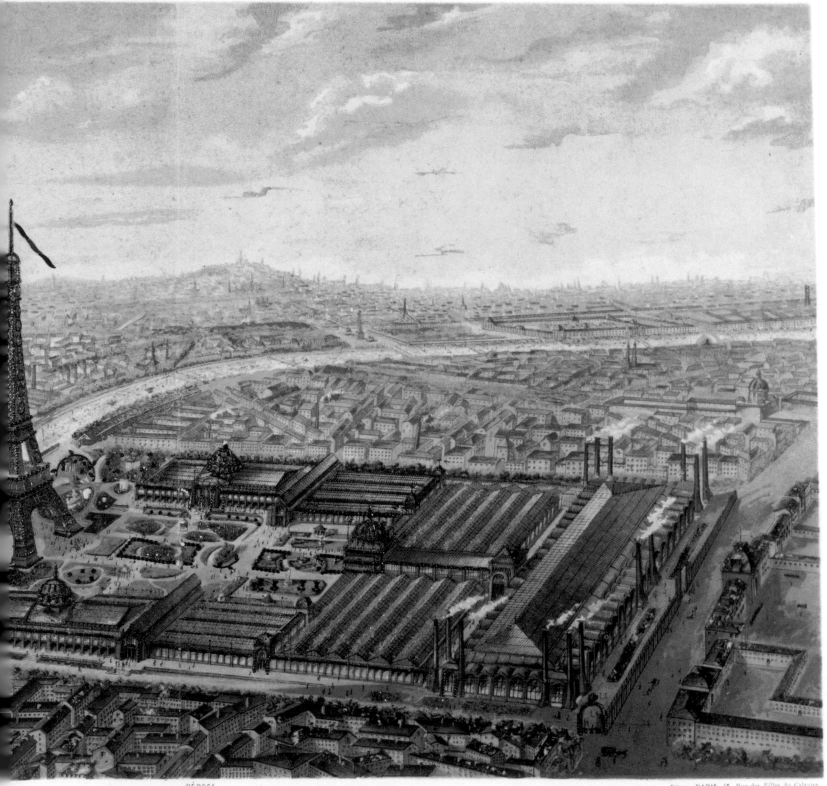

DÉPOSÉ

Déror: PARIS, 15, Rue des Filles du Calvaire.

POSITION UNIVERSELLE & INTERNATIONALE DE PARIS 1889.

# La Belle Epoque – 1890–1913

Art Nouveau, an artistic movement characterized by arabesques and floral and vegetative motifs, blossomed from 1890 to 1905. The rise of the associated architectural style was meteoric, thanks to the competition for the most beautiful façade in Paris, organized annually from 1898 onwards. The 1902 decree permitted an increase in the height and volume of façades, giving architects plenty of freedom to add domes, bow windows and decorative sculptures. Hector Guimard (1867–1942) won the first prize for façades in 1898 for his masterpiece, Castel Béranger at 14 rue La Fontaine in the 16th arrondissement. Jules Lavirotte received the prize in 1901 for his spectacular building at 29 rue Rapp in the 7th arrondissement, which was finished with glazed stoneware made by the ceramist Alexandre Bigot. Lavirotte won a second time in 1905 for the Céramic Hôtel at 33 Avenue de Wagram in the 8th arrondissement.

La Belle Epoque was the golden age of cabarets and cafés playing live music. Le Chat Noir, the Moulin Rouge and Le Lapin Agile in the 9th and 18th arrondissements of Montmartre were among 300 such establishments that flourished in the city.

In 1881, Rodolphe Salis (1851–1897) set up Le Chat Noir cabaret at 84 Boulevard de Rochechouart. He followed this with a branch at 12 rue Victor-Massé in 1885. Although this would close two years later, it would achieve posterity through the inspiration it provided for Aristide Bruant's song, which begins: "I seek my fortune all through Le Chat Noir".

The Moulin Rouge at 94 Boulevard de Clichy, headed by Joseph Oller and Charles Zidler in 1889, sported a façade topped by a red windmill designed by Adolphe Willette. This dance hall's main attraction was the French can-can. Performed by Jane Avril, nicknamed La Goulue or "the greedy one", the can-can inspired paintings and posters by Henri de Toulouse-Lautrec.

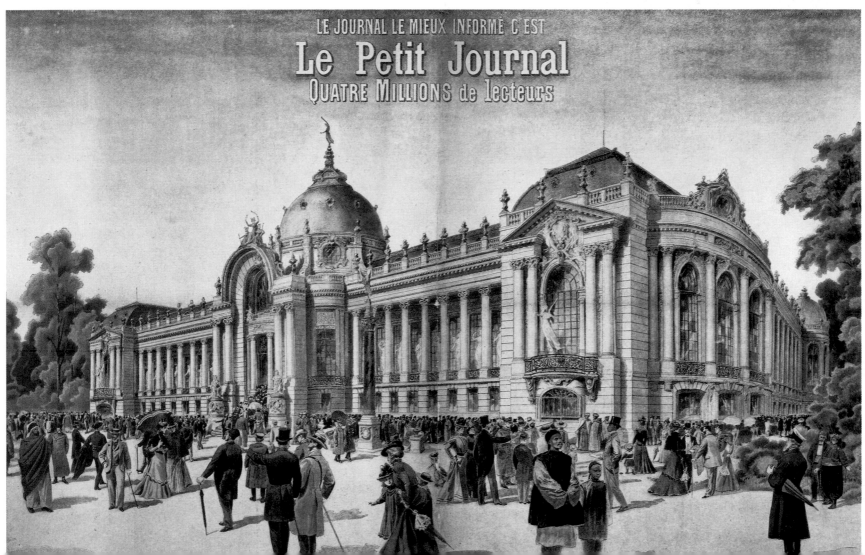

LE JOURNAL LE MIEUX INFORMÉ C'EST

# Le Petit Journal

QUATRE MILLIONS de lecteurs

Similarly, in Montmartre the artists' studios in the house at 13 Place Émile-Goudeau (dubbed the "wash-shed", probably by the poet Max Jacob) hosted the painters Juan Gris and Auguste Herbin, the sculptor Otto Freundlich and the poet Pierre Reverdy. Pablo Picasso was an intermittent resident from 1904 to 1912. It was in a studio there that he painted the seminal Cubist work, *Les Demoiselles d'Avignon* in 1907.

On 28 December 1895, the first public screening in front of a paying audience marked the emergence of an exciting invention with a great future: cinema. In the Salon Indien of the Grand Café at 14 Boulevard des Capucines in the 9th arrondissement, 33 spectators were to discover the films of the brothers, Auguste and Louis Lumière: *Workers Leaving the Lumière Factory in Lyon*, *Arrival of a Train at a Station* and *Baby's Dinner*.

In 1900, the Exposition Universelle (World's Fair), the fifth organized in Paris, was opened on 14 April by President Émile Loubet. The spectacular event called for new infrastructure (railway stations, a metro and a bridge) and buildings to accommodate 51 million visitors. Stations such as the Gare d'Orsay, designed by Victor Laloux, and the Gare des Invalides, a work by Juste Lisch, were constructed. During this time alterations were also carried out as Marius Toudoire oversaw renovations to the Gare de Lyon from 1895 to 1901.

**ABOVE** This painted steel sign for Le Chat Noir was created by Adolphe Willette (1857–1926). It was mounted above the entrance to the cabaret of the same name, which was open from 1881 until 1897, firstly at 84 Boulevard de Rochechouart and then at 12 rue Victor-Massé.

**RIGHT** A poster designed by Henri de Toulouse-Lautrec (1864–1901) to advertise Miss Eglantine's troupe at the Moulin Rouge. In 1896 Jane Avril asked Toulouse-Lautrec to portray her dancing this quadrille called "Troupe de Mademoiselle Églantine" with Églantine, Cléopâtre and Gazelle.

Troupe
M^LLE ÉGLAN

Eglantine
Jane Avril

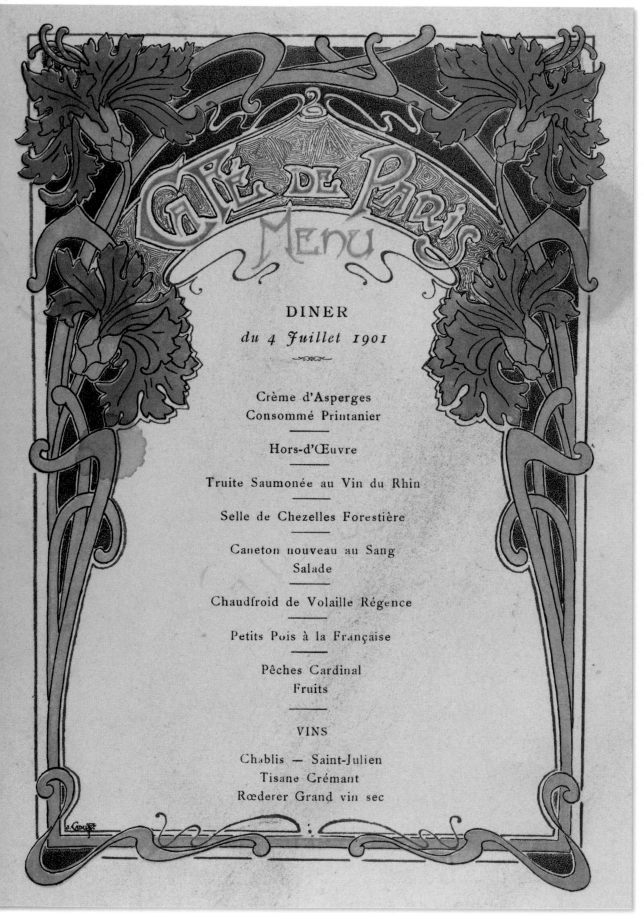

## CAFÉ DE PARIS

### Menu

**DINER**

*du 4 Juillet 1901*

Crème d'Asperges
Consommé Printanier

———

Hors-d'Œuvre

———

Truite Saumonée au Vin du Rhin

———

Selle de Chezelles Forestière

———

Caneton nouveau au Sang
Salade

———

Chaudfroid de Volaille Régence

———

Petits Pois à la Française

———

Pêches Cardinal
Fruits

**VINS**

Chablis — Saint-Julien
Tisane Crémant
Rœderer Grand vin sec

A menu from the Café de Paris for dinner on 4 July 1901. The Café de Paris opened in 1878 at 41 Avenue de l'Opéra (2nd arrondissement) and closed its doors in 1956. In the nineteenth century the use of menus became widespread, whereas it had previously been considered unnecessary, as the different dishes were presented to each guest.

**OPPOSITE** Pages from *The Masters of Fashion*, a catalogue published circa 1909 by M. Weeks with illustrations after designs by Fernand Toussaint (1873–1955). Monsieur Weeks, established at 1 rue Ambroise Thomas, in the 9th arrondissement, manufactured featherbones which were used to make collars, hats and corsets, in particular. He commissioned an advertising catalogue from the Belgian artist Fernand Toussaint. The painter had women posing in long robes with the tight waists that were then fashionable. In the early twentieth century, elegant women wore a corset which flattened the stomach by compressing it, crushing the kidneys and pushing the bust forward, in order to create a silhouette arched like an "S". The featherbones produced by Weeks had a pliable quality that was much appreciated by couturiers established around the fashion centre – rue de la Paix and Place Vendôme. Their comments are reproduced under the illustrations.

REDFERN

LAFERRIÈRE

Between 1897 and 1900, Pont Alexandre III was constructed by the engineers Jean Resal and Amédée Alby, in collaboration with the architects Cassien-Bernard and Gaston Cousin. The bridge linked the Gare des Invalides to the Champs-Elysées district. On 7 October, Nicholas II, Tsar of Russia, laid the foundation stone of the bridge, which was dedicated to his father Alexander III in honour of the alliance between France and Russia.

Nearby, two remarkable buildings were erected on either side of Avenue Winston Churchill: the Grand Palais, to accommodate temporary exhibitions, and the Petit Palais, as a municipal museum. The Grand Palais has a vast glass and iron nave, having been built by Albert Louvet, Henri Deglane and Albert Thomas, under the supervision of Charles Girault during 1896–1900, and Girault was the leading architect on the Petit Palais from 1897 until 1900.

Over the course of the World's Fair, Auguste Rodin (1840–1917) exhibited 150 sculptures in a pavilion on Place de l'Alma in the 8th arrondissement, which enhanced his reputation and brought him commissions from private clients, as well as European and American museums. The sculptor left his entire body of work to the French State, including *The Thinker*, *The Gates of Hell*, his art collections and his townhouse at 77 rue de Varenne in the 7th arrondissement, which today houses the museum dedicated to his art.

On 14 January 1913, the Gustave Moreau Museum at 14 rue de La Rochefoucauld in the 9th arrondissement opened its doors. At this residence, the Symbolist artist Gustave Moreau (1826–1898) lived and worked from 1852 until his death. The museum allows the opportunity to discover his elegant body of work, which is haunted by the theme of *Orpheus*.

**LEFT** A painting by Jean Béraud (1849–1936) of workers leaving the Paquin fashion house, around 1900. Pacquin's was based at 3 rue de la Paix (2nd arrondissement) and gave out onto the Place Vendôme, which was ornamented by the Vendôme column.

**ABOVE** The Alexander III Bridge.

**RIGHT** The entrance to the Abbesses Metro Station (Place des Abbesses, 18th arrondissement). Covered with a glass canopy, this entrance, designed by Guimard, was situated until 1970 at the Hôtel de Ville Station in front of rue Lobau in the 4th arrondissement.

# THE METRO

The capital set up a metro system in the late 1890s. The engineer Fulgence Bienvenüe (1852–1936) was given the task of completing the first six lines in 1898. On 19 July 1900, Line 1 served eight stations, including Champs Elysées-Clémenceau, which led to one of the World's Fair entrances. Between 1900 and 1913, Guimard designed the entrances to the Metro, which are superb examples of Art Nouveau, with their long, green metal stems and red glass flowers.

# The Inter-War Period

The assassination of Archduke Ferdinand, the heir to the Austrian Empire, in Sarajevo in Bosnia on 28 June 1914 triggered the outbreak of the First World War. On 3 August, Germany declared war on France.

After three bombs were dropped on Paris on 30 August, French troops were transported to the front by Parisian taxis, which had been requisitioned. The Battle of the Marne then took place during 6–9 September, a famous military action that resulted in the Anglo-French armies pushing the Germans back to the Ardennes.

The population of Paris had all its food supplies, electricity and coal rationed, and was ravaged by Spanish flu. The people endured aerial bombardments and shelling from a cannon nicknamed "Big Bertha". Georges Clemenceau, "the Father of Victory", signed the Treaty of Versailles on 28 June 1919, putting an end to hostilities for 20 years.

On 19 April 1919, the National Assembly voted to decommission the Thiers *enceinte* (defensive ring). The wall's demolition moved at a slow pace, as the surrounding grassy embankments were taken over by the sheds of rag-and-bone men. In 1922, the City built the first social housing there, equipped with facilities and services, such as baths and showers, day nurseries for children and wash-houses. Public gardens were laid out on the Boulevards des Maréchaux, the ring road of broad avenues built in place of the Thiers *enceinte*.

On Boulevard Jourdan, André Honnorat, with the backing of the industrialist Émile Deutsch de la Meurthe, founded the Cité Internationale Universitaire in 1920, an international campus modelled on a garden city by Lucien Bechmann. This accommodates 6,000 students from 120 countries in 37 picturesque residences in the centre of a 34-hectare (84-acre) park.

Young artists such as Pablo Picasso, Marc Chagall, Jules Pascin and Amedeo Modigliani sought new forms of plastic expression, and groups such as the Cubists, Fauvists, Surrealists and the School of Paris grew up. From 1900, the avant-garde artists gathered around the Boulevards Raspail and Montparnasse in the 14th arrondissement, a district where flats were affordable. At cafés such as La Closerie des Lilas, the Dôme and La Coupole, the painters met writers such as Ernest Hemingway, Blaise Cendrars, Jean Cocteau, Louis Aragon and André Breton, forming a cosmopolitan club that would become world-famous.

**ABOVE RIGHT** A Marne taxi – number 2862 G7 – shown on a postcard in 1923.

**RIGHT** Paul Colin's publicity poster for La Revue Nègre, which is painted on plywood. Joséphine Baker is shown dancing the Charleston, wriggling her hips and smiling to promote her show.

**OPPOSITE** Jeanne Lanvin's bedroom designed by Armand-Alber Rateau in 1925. The blue scheme comes from the the fashion designer Jeanne Lanvin's town house – 16 rue Barbet de Jouy (7th arrondissement) – which was demolished in 1965.

Parisians enthusiastically welcomed jazz, which had been introduced by American soldiers after the Great War. This music was all the rage in cabarets such as L'Abbaye de Thélème, located at 1 Place Pigalle. Performed in the Théâtre des Champs-Elysées, the famous Revue Nègre featured 12 musicians, including Sidney Bechet, who accompanied the star dancer, Joséphine Baker.

In 1925, the International Exhibition of Modern Industrial and Decorative Arts was held, with the aim of estabishing a central role for the applied arts. The pure geometric lines and modern furniture of Ruhlmann's pavilion attracted the attention of many visitors. The bedroom by Jeanne Lanvin is further evidence of this craze for interior design. Paris dominated the fashion world at that time with the collections of Coco Chanel and Madeleine Vionnet. Then, after 1935, the fashions of Edward Molyneux and Elsa Schiaparelli became influential.

Reconstruction work did not begin in Paris until 1930, partly because priority was given to restoring the devastated regions of north-east France at this time. During this period, official buildings were completed, such as the Marine Ministry in the 7th arrondissement, the main telephone exchange designed by François Le Coeur, and the Institute of Art and Archaeology in the 6th arrondissement. The introduction of concrete enabled the building of structures as varied as the Sainte-Odile Church in the 17th arrondissement, the Salvation Army refuge in the 13th arrondisement, the villas of Le Corbusier and the townhouses in rue Mallet-Stevens in the 16th arrondissement. In 1933, the economic crisis was deepening, and antipathy towards the parliamentary system was on the rise, fuelled by financial scandals, such as the Stavisky Affair in 1934. The Popular Front coalition won the elections in April and May 1936. For the first time in the history of the Third Republic, Léon Blum headed a socialist government. Faced with strikes on an unprecedented scale, Blum negotiated the Matignon Accords on 7 June 1936. The law that introduced the 40-hour week and a fortnight of paid holidays aroused great hopes in

the working class. However, the strikes delayed preparations for the International Exhibition dedicated to Art and Technology in Modern Life, which opened as the plasterwork was still drying on 24 May 1937.

All that remains of this event is the Palais de Tokyo, dedicated to contemporary art, and the Palais de Chaillot in the 16th arrondissment. The latter was built on the site of the old Palais du Trocadéro and designed by Léon Azéma, Louis-Hippolyte Boileau and Jacques Carlu. Its central rotonda, which was partly destroyed, is covered by the Esplanade of the Rights of Man. The two wings, which are twice the size of the old ones, end in two pavilions, which house the naval museum, the Musée National de la Marine; the ethnology museum, the Musée de l'Homme; and the design museum, the Cité de l'Architecture et du Patrimoine.

Also inside is the Théâtre National de Chaillot, designed by the Niermans brothers, which achieved fame with the performances of actor and director Jean Vilar. Roger Expert created the garden, which was augmented by ponds, waterfalls and sculptures.

On 1 September 1939, the German army invaded Poland, on the order of its leader Adolf Hitler, shattering the Treaty of Versailles. Two days later, the President of the Council and Minister of War, Édouard Daladier, declared hostilities against Germany: it was the start of the Second World War.

**OPPOSITE ABOVE** The Hotel Martel which was built by Rob Mallet-Stevens at 10 rue Mallet-Stevens in the 16th arrondissement in 1924–26. The building is characterized by the assembly of simple cube shapes structured around a cylinder shape.

**OPPOSITE BELOW** The official tribune, comprising Léon Blum, Roger Salengro and Marcel Cachi, is photographed being welcomed by the crowd in the Place de la Bastille on 14 July 1936.

**BELOW** A painting by Edouard Devambez of the Exposition Universelle (World's Fair) of 1937.

# Paris from 1939 to 1969

On 3 September 1939, France declared war on Germany after it invaded France's ally, Poland, on 1 September. On 14 June 1940, German soldiers marched into Paris, forcing it to be abandoned by French troops, and declared it an "open city". The French government wanted to prevent Paris from suffering the same fate as Warsaw, which had been destroyed entirely by the German air force, or Rotterdam, which was bombed even after the city had capitulated. After signing the armistice establishing the defeat of France on 22 June 1940 at Rethondes, the German Chancellor Hitler travelled to the capital the next day. On 10 June 1940, Marshal Petain was elected Chief of the French State in Vichy.

The persecution of Jews in Paris began in October 1940: they had to register in a census, wear the yellow star from May 1942 and were dispossessed of all their property. Large-scale raids were organized, including the round-up of Jews on 16 and 17 July 1942 at the "Vel d'Hiv" (an abbreviation for the Vélodrome d'Hiver, the Winter Velodrome), which resulted in the arrest of 13,000 Jews, who were then transported to the extermination camp at Auschwitz. A total of 50,000 Parisian Jews were deported and killed in the concentration camps.

In spite of danger and repression, resistance networks developed in order to continue the War. As the Allied armies under the command of General Eisenhower were approaching the capital, resistance groups launched an uprising against the occupiers from 19 until 24 August 1944. On forcing the agreement of the Americans, General Leclerc set off to liberate Paris with the 2nd French armoured division, while a detachment led by Captain Dronne entered the capital via Porte d'Italie on 24 August 1944.

**OPPOSITE BELOW** Second World War street signs in German on the Place de l'Opéra in the 9th arrondissement in 1944.

**LEFT** The terms of surrender signed by General von Choltitz, the German Commander-in-Chief of Paris, on 25 August 1944. General von Choltitz signed the terms of surrender in the billiard room of the Chief of Police's quarters. The document was also signed by General Leclerc and Colonel Henri Rol-Tanguy, the regional commander of the FTP-FFI (French resistance forces).

**ABOVE** Celebrations for the liberation of Paris on 26 August 1944 on the Place de L'Etoile-Charles de Gaulle. General de Gaulle, the head of the provisional government of the French Republic, gets ready to walk down the Champs-Elysées.

The following day, on 25 August, the German commander in Paris, General von Choltitz, signed the surrender of German troops in the police headquarters. On 26 August, General Charles de Gaulle, the President of the Provisional Government of the French Republic, walked down the Champs-Élysées and made the famous pronouncement at the Hôtel de Ville: "Paris abused! Paris destroyed! Paris tortured! But Paris liberated!"

After the resignation of General de Gaulle in 1946, the Fourth Republic was established (1947–58), with Vincent Auriol governing as President from 1947 to 1954, followed by Vincent Coty from 1954 to 1958. The first President of the ensuing Fifth Republic was General de Gaulle from 1959 to 1969.

Historians called the years from 1944 to 1974 the "Thirty Glorious Years", based on a period of economic growth, interrupted only by the oil crisis in 1974. In order to ease the critical shortage of housing, a massive construction project was started. More relaxed town planning regulations made it possible to develop much-needed, densely built areas, with structures reaching heights of up to 30 m (100 ft) in the city centre, and 37 m (120 ft) in the suburbs, and even higher in special cases of tall buildings. The tower at 31 rue Croulebarbe in

the 13th arrondissement, built by Edouard Albert in 1960, at a height of 67 m (220 ft), marked the beginning of a series of towers that would proliferate in outlying districts after 1967. These structures included Front de Seine, located in the 15th arrondissement.

In 1963, General de Gaulle inaugurated the Maison de Radio France at 116 Avenue du Président-Kennedy in the 16th arrondissement. Designed by Henry Bernard, the building is characterized by its round structure, finished with a 68-m (223-ft) high tower. To stem the rising tide of traffic, express routes opened up: the motorway approach to the south in 1960, the expressway on the Right Bank in 1967 and the *périphérique* ring road from 1956 to 1973, on the site of the Thiers *enceinte* (defensive ring). In 1962, faced by these upheavals in the urban landscape, the Minister of Culture passed a law to protect the historic quarters of the city: the Marais and Faubourg Saint-Germain in Paris.

The events of May 1968 began with a student revolt on 3 May. Students started to riot against the forces of law and order in the Latin Quarter, where they erected barricades. They occupied the Sorbonne, followed by the city's other universities. On 13 May, the revolt spread to the other social classes, precipitating the start of a general strike that

**ABOVE** A painting by Léonard Foujita (1886–1968) of a bistro in 1958. The painter has captured the ambience of the cafés frequented by students.

**ABOVE** Radio France House, which was built by Henry Bernard in 1963 at 116 Avenue du Président-Kennedy, in the 16th arrondissement.

**LEFT** The ceiling of the Opéra Garnier, painted by Marc Chagall (1887–1985).

would paralyze the country. On 27 May, the trade unions, bosses and government signed what became known as the Grenelle Accords at the Ministry of Labour at 127 rue de Grenelle in the 7th arrondissement: they increased the minimum wage and allocated more paid holidays, leading to a return to business as usual in France.

On 30 May, General de Gaulle gave the order to dissolve the National Assembly. The general election that followed secured a large majority for his party. The opposition movement had frittered out by the final night of rioting on 11 June 1968. The following year, the President resigned after the failure of the government's referendum on regionalization.

**OPPOSITE** Barricades that were built in May 1968 on the Boulevard Saint-Michel level with the rue des Écoles in the 5th arrondissement.

**ABOVE** A political poster entitled "The struggle continues", from 1968. This poster was produced by the studio of the fine art school, l'Ecole des Beaux-Arts, in May 1968. Around this time some 500 political posters were created, most of them anonymously, though some were signed by famous artists like Jean Hélion and Pierre Alechinsky.

# The Builder Presidents

**P**residents Georges Pompidou, who held power from 1969 until 1974; Valéry Giscard d'Estaing, from 1974 to 1981; François Mitterrand, from 1981 to 1995; and Jacques Chirac, from 1995 to 2007, were all very keen to leave their mark on the capital by commissioning museums and monuments.

In 1969, President Georges Pompidou appointed Richard Rogers (1933–) and Renzo Piano (1937–) to design an avant-garde multicultural institution, the Centre Georges Pompidou, at 102 rue Saint Martin in the 4th arrondissement. The architects came up with the concept of a giant Meccano set. The result that stands today is the Centre Pompidou, housing a modern art museum, a library and a space dedicated to contemporary music and cinema. The museum was inaugurated by President Valéry Giscard d'Estaing in 1977, three years after Pompidou's death.

Valéry Giscard d'Estaing decided to set up a museum of science, technology and industry, alongside a large park and musical facilities in 1976, on the site of the old abattoir at La Villette.

Adrien Fainsilber (1932–) was given the job of building the Cité des Sciences et de l'Industrie at 30 Avenue Corentin Cariou in the 19th arrondissement, which was opened by President François Mitterand on 13 March 1986, to celebrate the passage of Halley's comet. In 1985, Fainsilber collaborated with the engineer, Gérard Chamayou, on the Géode at 26 Avenue Corentin Cariou, which houses the IMAX cinema.

In 1977, Giscard d'Estaing originated the idea of converting the former Gare d'Orsay station into a museum. The project was entrusted to the architects Renaud Bardon, Pierre Colboc and Jean-Paul Philippon, and the interior design was assigned to Gae Aulenti. In 1986, François Mitterrand, Giscard d'Estaing's successor, opened the Musée d'Orsay at 1 rue de la Légion d'Honneur in the 7th arrondissement, and also the Science Museum in the Parc de la Villette in the 19th arrondissement. The Musée d'Orsay exhibits Western art from 1848 to 1914, including the Impressionist paintings of Monet, Manet, Pissarro and Degas.

**OPPOSITE ABOVE** The Georges Pompidou Centre, 102 rue Saint-Martin, 4th arrondissement. At 166 m (544½ ft) long and 45.5 m (149¼ ft) tall, the façade looking out on the square is made of metal and glass and enlivened by a large red escalator.

**ABOVE** The great gallery of the Musée d'Orsay. The museum houses works dating from 1848 to 1914, the period between the Louvre collections and those of the Georges Pompidou Centre.

**LEFT** The Geode, 26 Avenue Corentin Cariou, 19th arrondissement. The Geode, a sphere with a diameter of 26.5 m (120 ft), it is covered with mirrors made of polished steel and stands next to the Cité des Sciences et de l'Industrie (the Science and Industry City).

François Mitterand instigated the building of several new monuments. In 1981, he decided to turn the entire Louvre Palace into a museum. The offices of the Ministry of Finance, which occupied the Napoléon III Wing of the Louvre, were transferred to a ministry building at 1 Boulevard de Bercy in the 12th arrondissement, built by Borja Huidobro and Paul Chementov in 1989. This provided room for more galleries in the Louvre, which were used to display collections previously held in store. In 1989, Ieoh Ming Pei designed a transparent glass pyramid in the Napoleon Courtyard, which acts as the main entrance to the museum.

During this period, there was also significant investment in musical facilities. In 1989, a second opera house built by Carlos Ott, complementing the Opéra Garnier, opened its doors at 2 Place de la Bastille in the 12th arrondissement, while the musical venues in Parc de la Villette were completed in 1995, boosting the cultural development of Paris's eastern side.

Christian de Portzamparc (1944–) built the Cité de la Musique with two wings in the Parc de la Villette. The east wing contains a concert hall, a media library and a museum, the Musée de la Musique, at 221 Avenue Jean-Jaurès in the 19th arrondissement. The west wing, located at 211 Avenue Jean-Jaurès, houses the national conservatory for music and dance, the Conservatoire National Supérieur de Musique et de Danse de Paris, founded in 1795.

**OPPOSITE ABOVE** The Conservatoire National Supérieur de Musique (the National Superior Conservatory of Music), 211 Avenue Jean-Jaurés, 19th arrondissement, was built by Christian de Portzamparc.

**OPPOSITE BELOW** The July column and the Opéra de la Bastille on the Place de la Bastille.

**LEFT** A detail of the south façade of the Institute of the Arab World at 1 rue des Fossés-Saint-Bernard, in the 5th arrondissement. Inspired by Arab architecture, the south façade comprises 240 aluminium panels that mimic traditional Arab grilling. These panels are composed of diaphragms which open and close automatically by the hour.

**BELOW** Reaching a height of 20.6 m (67½ ft) and resembling the pyramid of Giza in Egypt (which is 21.65 m [71 ft] high), the Louvre Pyramid is composed of 673 glass lozenges.

# THE LOUVRE MUSEUM

The Louvre is the largest museum in the world in terms of its surface area and the number of visitors it welcomes each year. Originally a royal palace, it has housed a museum since 1793. The collections include Oriental, Egyptian, Greek, Etruscan and Roman art. They are complemented by Islamic art and Western painting, sculpture and drawing, ranging from the Middle Ages until 1848. There are around 35,000 exhibits in the permanent exhibition halls, including ancient Greek statues such as the *Venus de Milo* and the *Winged Victory of Samothrace*. The Louvre also contains the Italian Renaissance masterpiece *Mona Lisa* by Leonardo da Vinci, one of the most famous portraits in the history of art.

**ABOVE** The main façade of the Musée du Quai Branly (37 Quai Branly, 7th arrondissement). The main façade is enlivened by 26 boxes of varying sizes and colours which evoke the idea of huts perched in trees.

**OPPOSITE ABOVE** The Stravinsky Fountain, Place Igor-Stravinsky, 4th arrondissement. Conceived in 1983 by Jean Tinguely (1925–91) and Niki de Saint Phalle (1930–2002), it ilustrates the themes that were dear to the heart of the composer of the "Rite of Spring".

**OPPOSITE BELOW** The Simone de Beauvoir footbridge, built in 2006 by Dietmar Feichtinger, links the 12th and 13th arrondissements. On the right are the tower blocks of the National Library of France.

Jean Nouvel, Pierre Soria and the Architecture Studio built the Institut du Monde Arabe at 1 rue des Fossés-Saint-Bernard in the 5th arrondissement in 1987, with the aim of introducing people to the culture and civilization of the Arab World.

Meanwhile, the Bibliothèque Nationale (National Library) at 56 rue de Richelieu in the 2nd arrondissement, had outgrown its premises as a result of the growth in printed media during the twentieth century. Plans for a second site were drawn up to house its material and the Bibliothèque Nationale de France, designed by Dominique Perrault, opened its doors to readers in 1996 at Quai François Mauriac in the 13th arrondissement.

President Jacques Chirac wanted to establish a cultural centre dedicated to the civilization of Africa, Asia, Oceania and the Americas. Designed by Jean Nouvel, the Musée du Quai Branly opened near the Eiffel Tower, at 37 Quai Branly, in the 7th arrondissement. Modelled on the geographical origins of the "Arts Premiers", the Musée du Quai Branly houses a museum with about 300,000 objects, along with a cultural centre, and research and teaching facilities.

During the latter part of the twentieth century, commercial and industrial sites were repurposed as park areas, surrounded by shopping centres or apartment buildings. These included the Forum des Halles and gardens on the site of the Baltard Pavilions, which were demolished in 1971, and the Bercy and André-Citroën parks, in the 12th and 15th arrondissements respectively.

# Paris in the Twenty-First Century

The capital city enjoys a unique status, thanks to government reforms dating to 31 December 1975, which created two separate authorities: the Paris commune and the Paris département. The Mayor and Council of Paris govern the city: the ruling body includes 109 elected representatives, known as the Paris councillors.

Today, the city is divided into 20 arrondissements, each with a locally elected mayor, who is answerable to the Mayor of Paris. The council of each arrondissement plays a consultative role, boosted in 2002 by the district councils, and is a driving force in local life.

In its capacity as a département, Paris falls under the authority of the Prefect of Paris and the Île-de-France region. Uniquely, it is the Prefect of Police (appointed by the President of the Republic), who controls the city police. Jacques Chirac was elected Mayor from 1977 to 1995, Jean Tibéri from 1995 to 2001, and then Bertrand Delanoë in 2001, who was re-elected in 2008.

Bertrand Delanoë has taken steps to reduce the pollution caused by traffic and to promote the use of public transport. The covering of the *périphérique* ring road, started at Portes des Lilas, Brancion and Vanves, will be continued. The extension of the route will open up access to outlying areas, encouraging more development. The tram system, in operation since 2006 on the Boulevards des Maréchaux, promises to alleviate traffic on this through-route. In 2007 the city introduced a self-service bicycle system, known as the "Vélib". The scheme hires out 20,000 bicycles, and has proved a great success, attracting around 200,000 subscribers a year.

The city stages cultural events, such as the "Nuit Blanche" (White Night) and fun activities like "Paris Plages" (Paris Beaches). Since 2002, from 20 July to 20 August, recreational and sporting activities have been organized on the Right Bank of the Seine and on artificial beaches on La Villette Canal Basin.

The city's monumental heritage has been maintained thanks to a number of control measures. More than 1,000 monuments, townhouses and flats have been preserved under legislation for historical monuments, dating back to 1913. The Malraux law, passed in 1962, provided supplementary protection by designating 310 acres (126 hectares) of the Marais and 420 acres (171 hectares) of the Faubourg Saint-Germain "safeguarded sectors". The lower banks of the Seine, classed as "World Heritage sites" by UNESCO in 1994, offer unexpected views looking on to the riverbanks and the 37 bridges that cross the river.

There are many other splendid buildings with elegant interior décor. The Galerie Dorée (Golden Gallery) of the Banque de France is the jewel in the crown of the Hôtel de Toulouse. The gallery was entirely rebuilt during 1870–75 by Charles Questel, who modelled the restoration on François Mansart's design of 1640. Ten magnificent bas-reliefs, executed in 1715 by François-Antoine Vassé, were reinstated at that time. The naval themes and sculptures of hunting trophies refer to the roles of the Admiral of France and Grand Huntsman of France exercised by the Count of Toulouse, the legitimized son of Louis XIV.

The Musée Jacquemart-André, situated in the townhouse of its eponymous collectors and built in 1875 by Henri Parent, transports the visitor back into the eighteenth century. Private rooms display masterpieces by Greuze, Fragonard and Chardin, and a fresco by Tiepolo adorns the theatrical staircase in the winter garden.

**OPPOSITE** Paris Plage on Voie Georges Pompidou, photographed in 2009.

**ABOVE** The Musée Jacquemart-André, 158 Boulevard Haussmann, in the 8th arrondissement. The majestic double staircase is decorated with frescoes by Giambattista Tiepolo that were originally in the Villa Contarini near Venice in Italy.

**RIGHT** The gilded gallery of the Banque de France (Bank of France) at 31 rue Croix-des-Petits-Champs, in the 1st arrondissement. The Banque de France acquired the Hôtel de Toulouse in 1808. The paintings on the vaulted ceiling are copies of original frescoes by François Perrier.

ABOVE The Palais des Mirages (Mirage Palace) at the Musée Grevin, 10 Boulevard Montmartre, in the 9th arrondissement.

BELOW The tomb of Frederic Chopin in the Père-Lachaise Cemetery, 16 rue de Repos, in the 20th arrondissement.

The famous Reading Room built by Henri Labrouste in 1868 was the symbol of the Bibliothèque Nationale until 1996. Nine domes covered in ivory, enamelled squares are punctuated by a glass roof, which filters the daylight to create a subdued ambience. Sixteen iron slender columns give the space the feel of a basilica.

The Grévin Museum features a legendary attraction, the Palais des Mirages (Hall of Mirrors), which was devised by Eugène Hénard for the Exposition Universelle (World's Fair) in 1900. The mirror-filled room acts like an enormous kaleidescope, in which the play of lights conjures up the splendours of the palace of *One Thousand and One Nights*.

The north-east area of Paris remains disorienting because of its late urban development as a result of its unstable sub-soil and traditional avenues and factories. Montmartre Hill (the "Butte") stands out, with its winding roads, vines and wild and prolific vegetation, along with nearby villas along rue des Brouillards and Avenue Junot.

Each year, two million people visit the Père-Lachaise Cemetery in the 20th arrondissement, which was founded in 1804. They gather their thoughts at the graves of revolutionary heroes, marshals of the Empire, and in front of the Communards' Wall, the memorial to the 1871 Paris Commune. Veritable cults have grown up around the tombs of Héloïse and Abélard, Frédéric Chopin and Jim Morrison.

Walkers can choose from plenty of charming locales, such as the "Mulberry Courtyard" in the École des Beaux-Arts, the indoor garden of the Petit-Palais, or the Carpeaux Fountain in Place Camille Jullian. South-west of the city, in the 13th arrondissement, are the new buildings of the Avenue de France and the Université Paris Diderot, inaugurated in 2007, while the Quai and Port d'Austerlitz are undergoing major renovation work.

Recently, the magasins généraux, customs-bonded warehouses built in 1907, have been transformed by the architectural agency Jakob + MacFarlane, and promise to stimulate business beside the Institut Français de la Mode et du Design (the French Fashion and Design Institute). The city that is constantly reinventing itself has endless surprises in store for the pedestrian.

**RIGHT** This nightime view of the capital highlights the Champ de Mars, the Eiffel Tower and the Trocadéro Palace.

# INDEX

Page numbers in *italic* type refer to illustrations or their captions.

# FURTHER INFORMATION

## INTERNET

Mairie de Paris : paris.fr
Office du tourisme de Paris : parisinfo.com

## PRINCIPAL MUSEUMS

Maison de Victor Hugo, 6 Place des Vosges, 4th arrondissement
Musée Carnavalet, 23 rue de Sévigné, 3ème arrondissement
Musée d'Orsay, 1 rue de la Légion d'Honneur, 7th arrondissement
Musée du Louvre, Palais du Louvre, 1st arrondissement
Musée du Petit Palais, Avenue Winston Churchill, 8th arrondissement
Musée Picasso, 5 rue de Thorigny, 3rd arrondissement

## LIBRARY

Bibliothèque Historique de la Ville de Paris, 24 rue Pavée, 75004 Paris

## BIBLIOGRAPHY

*A Paris walking guide*, Paris, Parigramme, 2009.

Bos, Agnès, *Les églises flamboyantes de Paris*, Paris, Picard, 2003.

Bruson, Jean-Marie & Leribault, Christophe, *Peintures du musée Carnavalet, catalogue sommaire*. Paris, Paris-Musées, 1999.

Busson (Didier), *Paris ville antique*, Paris, éditions du Patrimoine (Guides archéologiques de la France), 2001.

Chadych, Danielle & Leborgne, Dominique, *Atlas de Paris*, Paris, Parigramme, 2007.

Chadych, Danielle, *Le Marais*, Paris, Parigramme, 2005.

Chadych, Danielle & Leborgne, Dominique, *Paris pour les nuls*, Paris, First, 2006.

Chadych, Danielle & Leborgne, Dominique, *Paris pour les nuls rive droite et rive gauche*, Paris, First, 2008.

*Dictionnaire du Grand Siècle*, ed. François Bluche, Paris, Fayard, 2005.

*Dictionnaire du Second Empire*, ed. Jean Tulard, Paris, Fayard, 1995.

Fierro, Alfred, *Histoire et dictionnaire de Paris*, Paris, Robert Laffont (Bouquins), 1996.

Gady, Alexandre, *Les hôtels particuliers de Paris*, Paris, Parigramme, 2008.

Gallet, Michel, *Les architectes parisiens du XVIIIe siècle*, Paris, Mengès, 1995.

Garrigues *La France du VIIe au XXe siècle à travers soixante et onze documents*, Paris, 1980, Archives nationales, Musée de l'Histoire de France.

Guicharnaud, Hélène, *Quand le Louvre raconte Paris*, Paris, Paris Musées, Musée du Louvre, 2005.

*Le Guide du promeneur de Paris*, Paris, Parigramme, 2007.

Hillairet, Jacques, *Dictionnaire historique des rues de Paris*, Paris, éditions de Minuit, 1979.

Leborgne, Dominique, *Saint-Germain des Prés et son faubourg*, Paris, Parigramme, 2005.

Levisse Touzé, Christine, *Paris libéré, Paris retrouvé*, Paris, Gallimard (Découvertes Gallimard Histoire), 1994.

*La Mémoire de la France, quarante ans d'enrichissement des Archives de France*, exposition organisée par la direction des Archives de France, préface par J. Favier, réalisation J.-D. Pariset, Hôtel de Rohan, février-avril 1994, Paris.

*Nouvelle histoire de Paris*, Paris, Association pour la publication d'une Histoire de Paris, 14 volumes.
*Paris, ballade au fil du temps*, Paris, Sélection du Reader's Digest, 2007.

*Paris, le guide du patrimoine*, sous la direction de Jean-Marie Pérouse de Montclos, Paris, Caisse nationale des monuments historiques et des sites, 1994.

*Les plans de Paris: des origines (1493) à la fin du 18è siècle*, catalogue collectif sous la direction de Jean Boutier, Paris, Bibliothèque nationale de France, 2003.

Rougerie, Jacques *Paris insurgé: la Commune de 1871 retrouvé*, Paris, Gallimard (Découvertes Gallimard Histoire), 2007.

Sandron, Dany & Lorentz, Philippe, *Atlas de Paris au Moyen Age*, Paris, Parigramme, 2006.

Tulard, Jean, Fierro, Alfred, & Fayard, Jean-François, *Histoire et dictionnaire de la Révolution française : 1789-1799*, Paris, Robert Laffont (Bouquins), 1996.

# PICTURE CREDITS